Paddy Doyle was born in Wexford in 1951 and now lives in Dublin. He is married with three grown up sons. He is recognized as a leading disability activist in Ireland and has been a member of the government-appointed Commission of the Status of People with Disabilities.

A frequent contributor to television, radio and the print media on matters as diverse as the role of the church in caring for children to the legalization of marijuana for medical use, he is currently Chief Executive of the National Representative Council – a body established to ensure that the rights of people with disabilities are upheld. He has also travelled extensively throughout Europe and the United States, speaking at conferences about disability and child sexual abuse.

Paddy Doyle was the first recipient of the Christy Brown Award for Literature, in 1984, for a television play entitled *Why do I Bother*. Shortly after it was first published, *The God Squad* became a bestselling book in both Ireland and the United Kingdom. It also won the *Sunday Tribune* Arts Award for Literature. In 1993 Paddy Doyle was awarded a Person of the Year Award for An Outstanding Contribution to Irish Society by the Rehab Group.

D0632451

Waterford Oct '03

Your Froggy

THE GOD SQUAD

Paddy Doyle

CORGI BOOKS

THE GOD SQUAD
A CORGI BOOK: 0 552 15027 4

Originally published in Great Britain by The Raven Arts Press

PRINTING HISTORY
Raven Arts Press edition published 1988
Corgi edition published 1989

19 20

Set in 10.5/13pt Sabon by
Phoenix Typesetting, Ilkley, West Yorkshire.

Corgi Books are published by Transworld Publishers,
61-63 Uxbridge Road, London W5 5SA,
a division of The Random House Group Ltd,
in Australia by Random House Australia (Pty) Ltd,
20 Alfred Street, Milsons Point, Sydney, NSW 2061, Australia,
in New Zealand by Random House New Zealand Ltd,
18 Poland Road, Glenfield, Auckland 10, New Zealand
and in South Africa by Random House (Pty) Ltd,
Endulini, 5a Jubilee Road, Parktown 2193, South Africa.

Printed and bound in Great Britain by Clays Ltd, St Ives plc.

For Eileen

PROLOGUE

For years I had believed my uncle to be dead. Attempts at correspondence, spanning over twenty years and including an invitation to my wedding in 1974, had failed to bring any response. So that Sunday in 1983 as I drove with my family from Dublin my feelings were of trepidation. The phone call telling me he was still alive and in hospital in Wexford had come about because of the media exposure surrounding my being awarded the first Christy Brown Award for Literature.

How was he going to react to me – or I to him? I was aware of going to see a man who was ill, but even more aware that he was the sole living relative I had – apart from my younger sister. He surely would give me the information I needed about my parents and my past.

On arrival at the hospital, crowds were lining the grounds for the removal of the remains of a local dignitary of the church. I left my wife and children in the car and moved through them, overhearing their comments about my appearance on *The Late Late Show* the previous night.

I was nervous and waited outside the ward before asking a senior nurse to tell him I had arrived, explaining to her who I was and the number of years that had elapsed since he and I had last met.

As soon as I entered the ward we recognized each other and he began to cry. He was in some pain following the removal of his appendix and obviously distressed at seeing me. After awkwardly discussing his health, I asked him about my parents. At first he ignored my questions about them and would only reply repeatedly 'You'll be all right when I'm gone'. Finally I forced him to tell me that my mother had died of 'the disease' but he just wept when asked about my father, avoiding the question in every way he could. Eventually he revealed where my mother was buried but still consistently refused to say anything about my father. When I asked about photographs he said there were none.

Back in Dublin the suspicion of a conspiracy of silence which I had long held was reinforced and I was convinced that whatever happened to my parents had been deliberately concealed from me by the silence of a whole society and time. I knew so little that I even began to wonder if the man I called 'uncle' could in fact be my father. I discussed what had happened with a doctor friend and we decided that there had to be a way of getting to the truth. I was a man with no past. There must be someone who knew why I was sent to an Industrial School and somebody who could explain the origins or cause of my disability. Previous attempts at such ventures had failed. What past I did have amounted to a birth and baptismal certificate. Enquiries about medical records had yielded no results. I had no reason to believe that things would be any different this time.

Yet gradually the truth began to filter through as the thirty year conspiracy of silence slowly cracked. Unexpectedly I learned of the deaths of both parents in a letter from someone who did know of my past. Though the information was scant it was filling great gaps. I began to delve further and with the help and support of my wife, I intensified my search.

I discovered that on the morning of August 15th, 1955, I was taken to the District Court in County Wexford, where I was found to be in possession of a guardian who did not exercise proper guardianship. Two days after my appearance an Order of Detention in a Certified Industrial School was drawn up and brought to the house I was staying in by a Garda for legal execution. The form was signed by the Justice of the Court. I was four years and three months old at the time.

In early June of that year my mother had died from cancer of the breast and six weeks later my father committed suicide by hanging himself from an alder tree at the back of a barn on a farm where he worked as a labourer. I was taken into court by a woman who was later described as 'a sort of an aunt'.

Earlier at the inquest into my father's death, my mother's brother who had lived with us had given a statement which I have in my possession. Part of it reads:

'I left the house at 8.15 a.m. this morning 15/7/1955. When I was leaving Patrick Doyle was in bed. On my return to the house this evening at 9.15 p.m. Patrick Doyle was not in the house. I looked around the back of the house and later went to the haggard where I found him with a rope around his neck hanging from an alder tree on the fence. I felt one of his hands and it was cold. His feet were about two feet off the ground.

'I didn't cut down the body. I sent word to the village with a little girl that was passing for someone to come down to me. Someone arrived in about 15 minutes. A priest from the nearby parish cut down the body. Since the deceased man's wife died about six weeks ago he has been worrying about her ever since. He was a labourer by occupation and about 52 years of age.'

A doctor had told the inquest that he had been called to the farm by the Gardai and after an examination had estimated that the time of death had been some twelve hours earlier. It appears that I witnessed the suicide and may have been found wandering on the farm in great distress.

It had taken me thirty years to discover the truth about the deaths of both my parents even though a death such as my father's was likely to have made the local, if not the national newspapers, of the time. With that in mind I searched through old copies of *The Wexford People* in the National Library. There in the July 1955 edition I read the details of my father's suicide, and the other events surrounding it. While searching through these papers I tried to find a death notice for my mother, but did not succeed. Reading a journalist's report of the event made me realize that this was not a secret, unheard of event, but a public domain issue.

I began to pressurize my uncle for photographs, certain there must be some and that he could tell me where to look. A letter arrived at my home, containing a short note and two photographs: one of myself with a group of children on my First Communion day, the other of two women and a child in a buggy. The child was me, and the woman standing behind was my mother. Until then I had no idea what my mother looked like. Though she had obviously been a part of my early life, I had no memory of her. At 35 years of age I was seeing my mother for the first time. I didn't cry, nor was I jolted in any way. Despite my best efforts I have as yet been unable to get a photograph of my father. I still have no idea of what he looked like, my only memories of him are those that haunted me as a child. A faceless man hanging dead. A fierce determination set in to get any information I could, which eventually resulted in my obtaining the original Order of Detention, rust marks from a paper clip etched on it, statements of witnesses given at the coroner's court and other papers pertaining to his death.

There were many times during the course of writing this book, that I questioned what I was doing, often frightened by the chill running through my body as I wrote. The support I received from people, particularly Eileen, my wife, was limitless. The impact of having to absorb one shock after another was at times very painful for her and she cried enough for both of us.

Many people familiar with the effects of institutional care, particularly Industrial Schools, will say that I have gone too easy on them. Lives have been ruined by the tyrannical rule and lack of love in such places. People have been scarred for life. Others will wonder why I bothered to delve into the past at all.

This book spans just six years of my life. There was almost consistent trauma, ranging from the death of both my parents, to the isolation of hospital wards and brain surgery. Such surgery was not just traumatic, but debilitating also. One procedure could not be completed because of the breakdown of the apparatus, prompting me to wonder why it was not attempted again when the apparatus was repaired.

It is important to point out that interspersed with this trauma were moments of great love and affection. From the gentle kiss of a young nurse to the soft hand of a caring nun. It may well be the case that these were the moments which preserved my sanity and gave me something to live for.

This book is not an attempt to point the finger, to blame, or even to criticize any individual or group of people.

Neither is it intended to make a judgement on what happened to me. It is about a society's abdication of responsibility to a child. The fact that I was that child, and that the book is about my life is largely irrelevant. The probability is that there were, and still are, thousands of 'mes'.

Paddy Doyle,
Dublin,
Sept. 1988.

CHAPTER ONE

I lay flat on my back on the narrow cast iron bed in the dormitory of St Michael's Industrial School in Cappoquin. The thin horse-hair mattress was barely adequate to separate my thin body from its taut criss-cross wire springs. My eyes were fixed on the ceiling, the paint flaking just above the bed. From a room below the sound of children singing seeped through the floorboards.

In the distance a train hooted, heralding its imminent arrival at the station just beyond the high granite walls of the school. I turned towards the tall sashed window a few feet from my bed. Through watery eyes I noticed the sun was shining, though the dormitory was cold and dark. The train hooted again, louder as it drew nearer the station, panting and hissing through the stillness of the day.

It had been three weeks since my uncle had driven me here in the black Morris Minor owned by his employer. In his pocket he carried the order of detention from the District Court in Wexford sentencing me to seven years in custody. The charge against me was of being found having a guardian who did not exercise proper guardianship. I was then four years and three months old. I remember being terrified of the nuns from the moment I entered the

Industrial School and clinging to my uncle, pleading with him to take me home. A tall, thin evil-looking nun had come towards me and forced my hand away from his before gripping my jumper at the neck to ensure that I could not grab hold of him again. I'd screamed and kicked in an attempt to free myself, but the more I struggled, the tighter her hold became. She told my uncle that I would settle down just as soon as he left. I can remember trying to get free of her and follow my uncle. But the nun held me firmly by the ear lobe and warned me to stop, otherwise I would receive a 'good flaking'.

Three weeks had taught me the meaning of that phrase. I rose cautiously from my bed, rubbed my eyes and cheeks with my knuckles and went towards the window. I stood back, frightened that I might be seen from the yard below. I moved as close to it as I felt it was safe to do.

The granite wall glistened in the sunlight like a million jewels. I pressed my face against the window and watched the approaching train. The sun shone onto its black rounded front like a spotlight. The shiny, black funnel belched out a mixture of smoke and steam that hung above the tender in a large plume of grey and white, and when the colours merged to black and soared into the sky the cloud cast a dark shadow across the grey concrete of the school yard. Behind the glossy tender, the wagons laden with sugar beet rattled along, zig-zagging awkwardly in contrast to the graceful, steady movement of the engine. A screeching of the wheels on the tracks and a loud prolonged hissing brought the engine to a halt. I noticed the sparks made by the wheels as they skidded along, igniting in the dark shadow of the underframe. A final banging of the wagons as each one buffeted into the one ahead of it, then silence. Total silence. Two men in blackened boiler suits jumped cautiously from the tender and stood briefly in the hot sunshine as both rubbed their foreheads with a sleeve. Before leaving the train each in turn slapped the great tender on its belly as a farmer would a cow, or a jockey a horse, a sign of affection, the beast had done her job well.

I counted the wagons as the tender took water from the great red-oxide tank overhead. There were fifteen, and a guard's van at the rear. Each one filled with sugar beet, mud baked by the combination of hot sun and drying breeze. The stillness of the moment was broken by a sudden rush of feet into the yard below the dormitory window. I backed away from the window though I still looked out as the other children ran about the yard screaming their excitement. Some of them tried to climb the wall to get a better view but their efforts were brought to an abrupt halt by the swish of a cane from one of the nuns patrolling the yard like a black shadow. One boy who was midway up the wall fell to the ground writhing in pain having felt the full force of Mother Paul's cane across his calf muscles. He lay curled up, on the ground screaming and gripping his leg tightly. The other boys stood still, frozen in terror.

I watched. I knew the pain of the bamboo and the horror of being beaten until it was no longer possible to stand it. As blow after blow landed, I trembled, fully convinced that I would receive similar punishment when Mother Paul came to the dormitory. I went back to bed and pulled the covers over my head in an attempt to escape the piercing, painful screams. Finally the screaming stopped. I lay waiting for the footsteps.

'Well, Master Doyle . . . are you finished now or would you prefer to spend more time here on your own?'

Startled by the sound of Mother Paul's voice, I turned down the bedcovers. Her tall black-clad figure stood beside my bed, her wrinkled hand carrying the cane that she kept partially hidden up the long loose sleeve of her habit. She stared coldly down at me, her icy-blue eyes seeming magnified through the thick lenses of her rimless spectacles. Her long pointed nose threatened to drip its watery contents onto my bed but was halted by the swift use of her check-coloured handkerchief. Her wicked-looking face was gripped tightly in the habit of the Sisters of Mercy. The black habit was pulled tight at the waist by a leather belt.

'Get up out of that bed then this instant,' she roared, 'and I don't want to hear another word from you about a man hanging from a tree. It's not good for the other children and, besides, people don't do that sort of thing.'

'But there was . . .'

The nun's mouth tensed visibly. 'That is enough, I warn you. Get dressed and get down to the assembly hall immediately.'

'Yes, Mother,' I said.

She left as I started to dress. Once I had my boots laced up I walked slowly through the dormitory stopping as I reached the door that led to the room where Mother Paul and Mother Michael slept. Gripped by curiosity, my eyes fixed on the large oak door with a big iron key protruding from its lock. On the tips of my boots I approached, gripped the key and turned it, trying to ensure it would make no sound. It clicked, the noise sounding much louder than it really was in the emptiness of the large room. I cupped the knob in my hands and turned it slowly before gently pushing the door open. I walked into the carpeted room, its whiteness glaring when compared to the drabness of the dormitory. Walls and ceiling were painted in a gloss white and the only thing hanging on the wall was a large wooden crucifix. On a press beside the white quilted beds was a statue of the Virgin Mary, a golden rosary beads entwined in her hands. I looked at the statue. Its pale blue eyes appeared to be watching my every move. I moved uneasily back out of the room, closing the door gently before locking it and walking down the wooden stairs to the assembly hall.

The hall was a big room with bare floorboards and large sashed windows that rattled whenever there was even the slightest breeze. The walls were wood-panelled and painted black to about three feet above floor level. The remainder was painted dark grey. The only furniture was two chairs which were used by the nun who was in charge of the children or by another nun who played the piano, thumping out chords and shouting at us to sing. In a sudden movement she would stop playing and jump to her feet, usually knocking her chair over as she did. Her finger wagged and in a voice that rose in pitch with each word she would say, 'There is a crow in amongst you and when I find out who it is he is going to have sore ears.'

'What kept you?' Mother Paul snapped. I hesitated before answering, 'I couldn't get my boots tied, there was a knot in the laces, Mother.'

'I sincerely hope that is the truth,' she leered.

'Yes, Mother.'

'Get over here and learn this song before Miss Sharpe comes back from her holidays, she will expect you all to know it.'

As I approached the piano she suddenly slapped me in the face.

'Where were you?'

I looked at her, surprised by the question and the sharpness in her voice.

'I asked you a question and when I ask someone a question I expect to get an answer. Is that clear?'

'Yes, Mother.'

'Now tell everyone where you were and why you were late.'

'I was in the dormitory.'

She slapped me viciously across the face again. Then at the top of her voice Mother Paul shouted, 'I was in the dormitory . . . What?'

'Mother,' I responded, my voice trembling. 'I was in the dormitory, Mother.'

'Louder,' she demanded.

'I was in the dormitory, Mother, then.'

'Why? Tell everyone why you were sent to the dormitory,' she demanded.

'For making up stories, Mother,' I said.

She hit me again.

'For telling lies, that's why. Is that the reason?'

'Yes, Mother.'

'What were the lies you were telling? I want everyone to hear.'

I could barely speak, my voice shook and tears welled in my eyes. My bottom lip quivered and I began to cry.

'Speak up, child,' she demanded.

'I said I saw a man hanging from a tree.'

I stood there shaking.

'This little pup is a liar,' Mother Paul said to the other frightened children as she held me by my ear. 'And everyone here knows what happens to people who tell lies.' There was silence.

'What happens to children who tell lies?' she asked.

'They go to hell,' they all answered. The nun smiled.

'Not only that,' she continued, 'but they burn in its flames for ever and ever. That is what is going to happen to this little liar. He is going to burn for ever in hell if he doesn't stop. Always remember to tell the truth.'

She pulled me over to the piano and struck the chords of a song I knew well, one which the nuns began to teach me shortly after I entered the school.

'Stop whinging immediately and sing,' Mother Paul ordered.

As I did my voice trembled. I stood straight, with my hands crossed in front of me as I had been taught to do whenever I was asked to sing for visitors. My voice was a pleasant boy-soprano type which the nuns appeared to take great pleasure demonstrating for visitors to the school.

> *'A Mother's Love is a blessing,*
> *No matter where you roam,*
> *Keep her while she's living,*
> *You'll miss her when she's gone,*
> *Love her as in childhood,*
> *Though feeble, old and grey,*
> *For you'll never miss a Mother's Love*
> *till she's buried beneath the clay.'*

Mother Paul waved her hand and the rest of the children joined in the remaining verses.

When we had finished singing Mother Paul reminded us that as we had no parents it fell to the nuns to give us the guidance and grace that would make us into fine young men. Nuns were married to God she said as she raised her right hand to show a thin silver ring. Nuns did not have children in the way mothers had. 'Each of you was sent to St Michael's by God and you will be trained in the manner He would like. Mark my words, you will all one day be proud to have been a part of this school.'

Two years after being admitted to St Michael's I had become familiar with its routine. The official report on me for that year says: 'A bright little lad. Made his first Holy Communion when barely over 6 years.' For the year 1958 the same report remarks: 'A very bright little boy, quiet

19

and intelligent. Able to serve Mass in the Parish Church. Promoted in school.' I found it easier to mix with the other children as each day passed and I joined in whatever games I could.

One day, as I heard the beet train pulling into the station I climbed the wall to get a better look at it and to see if I could get either the driver or the fireman to throw some sugar beet over. I shouted, and a lump of beet sailed over the wall, landing in the school yard. There was a rush to get it but I decided that as I was the one who had asked for it I should have it, and furthermore I would decide who I was going to share it with. Because the mud was so dry it was easy to remove from the beet. My efforts at breaking it up for distribution among my friends proved more difficult than I had expected. I put it on the ground and banged the heel of my boot down hard on it hoping it would break but it didn't. A jagged edge of the wall proved more useful. Soon lumps of beet were being scattered around the ground. Hungry grasping hands picked up the pieces and if they were small enough they were stuffed into waiting mouths. Those who did get some of it moved to a secluded part of the yard to suck and chew large bits of the creamy-coloured beet.

The group of which I was a part broke up. Mother Paul was coming towards me. The sun cast her long shadow on the ground as I dropped the beet I was eating. In one hand she had her cane and under the other arm she was carrying the school dog, a Jack Russell, called Toby. The dog barked and I froze, pressing my back hard against the wall. The dog barked again. I was terrified. I hated dogs. I wanted to run but I couldn't move. The long cane of Mother Paul pressed into my shoulder pinning me where I stood.

'Will you look at him,' she leered as the other children gathered around.

'This pup who is so brave when it comes to stealing from the train is afraid of his life of a tiny dog.'

She pointed to the dog, and as I attempted to run he growled. Mother Paul jeered. She told me that just as I had been created by God so had the dog, then she stroked his head gently and moved closer to me. I screamed with fright, causing the dog to growl and almost leap from her arms.

'Nice Toby,' Mother Paul said. 'Do you like this dog?' she asked.

'No, Mother.'

She hit me across the legs with her cane and I shrieked with pain. She hit me again. And seeing my fear she grinned. There was an evil look on her face.

'Say you like little Toby,' she ordered.

I paused for a minute, my fear gradually turning to rage. Mother Paul looked at me through slit eyes and purple thin lips. She hit out again. I ran towards her and kicked her as hard as I could across the shin. The crack of my boot echoed around the now silent yard. She grimaced and dropped the dog. It ran for cover as I ran across the yard. Before I could make my way into the assembly hall I was grabbed and held by another nun until Mother Paul arrived limping and red-faced. She held me by the ear and, as I tried to kick her again and again, she twisted it until I was almost motionless. She lashed out at me with her cane, hitting me across the back of the knees. I fell to the ground, screaming and writhing in agony.

'Get up off that ground, you filthy, dirty little pup,' she yelled. 'You will get what any little brat would get for kicking a holy nun. Mark my words, you will be sorry.' She ordered the rest of the children inside, shouting at them that the punishment I was going to get would ensure that none of them would do what I had done; kick a woman chosen by God to do His work.

In the assembly hall she looked around for somewhere to vent her anger. She ordered a group of children to bring her a table which was in one corner of the room. When it was placed to her satisfaction she addressed the rest of the boys while holding me firmly by my ear.

'This child,' she poked her cane into my ribs before continuing, 'is possessed by an evil demon.' She paused to allow the magnitude of what she had said to sink deep into the minds of the other children.

'He has the devil inside him and it is my duty to him and to God in Heaven to get it out. He must be punished and severely so. He must ask God for forgiveness for the terrible sin he has committed.' She ordered me to strip. I stood motionless. Mother Paul slammed her cane onto the table in front of her.

'Strip, child,' she shouted.

I began to take off my clothes. First my heavy grey jumper, then the grey shirt.

'Come on, come on, I haven't all day. Get those trousers, boots and socks off immediately.'

I stood there shivering, a combination of cold and fear. My ribs protruded through my skin as though I was under-nourished. My skin was white except for red patches where I had been hit or jabbed by the cane.

'Get onto that table,' she demanded.

I lay on it naked, allowing my arms to hang over its side until I was told to bring them onto the table and down either side of my body. She gazed at me, a perverse grin on her face.

'Roll over onto your face and let this be a lesson to you.'

Her long cane whistled through the air and in the moment before it made contact every muscle in my body tensed and I became rigid. I squirmed and the first vicious blow stung, but I did not cry out.

'Never, never, as long as you live must you assault a holy nun in that manner.'

A second, third and fourth painful lash of the bamboo, and I could feel my skin burning. For some reason I cannot understand I refused to cry out. The number of times I was struck increased until it was impossible to count, just as it was difficult to separate one blow from the next. I remained silent, until the pain became unbearable and I finally screamed. I was being struck everywhere from the back of my neck down to my heels.

'Now,' she said, 'the devil is coming out of him.' The ferocity and frequency of the blows lessened until eventually I rolled off the table and onto the floor. Mother Paul looked pleased.

'That is how to get the devil out of someone like him. Only Satan himself would make a child behave the way he did. It will be a long time before he'll kick a nun again. Stand up and get your clothes on immediately,' she yelled before warning the other boys that they would receive the same treatment if they didn't keep quiet. I dressed in the silence, the coarse bulls wool trousers hurting my legs as I pulled them on. When I was clothed she pulled me to her by my ear and told the other children that I was being put into the coal shed for the remainder of the day. She led me away, holding my ear tightly between her thumb and forefinger.

She fumbled through the pockets of her black habit for a key to fit the padlocked door. Impatiently, she undid the lock and threw the door open.

'Get in and stay there. Pray. Say an Act of Contrition so that God may forgive you.'

She slammed the door. In the darkness I could hear the bolt being slid across and the lock applied. I stood and listened to her footsteps fading.

In any other circumstances I would have been terrified of

the darkness. Now it came as a blessing, a place of refuge from the terror of my persecutor. I sat on the dusty black-ened floor and wept. The pain of the punishment was unbearable. My flesh stung, and though I could not see, I was certain my skin had blistered. I hated that nun, and I said it. I wished her damned in hell to burn for ever.

The only light that entered the coal shed was from under the door and through a cracked slate in the roof. I moved under this slit of light and stared at it, straining my eyes, until they became tired. Within minutes I was in a deep sleep. The darkness, the cold or the dampness didn't matter to me. Peace mattered.

A noise woke me. The rattle of keys mingled with the distinct sound of the long Rosary beads worn by the nuns. The light through the roof had gone grey and I guessed that it was evening. The chill evening air crept under the door making me feel cold. The bolt slapped back and the door was flung open. What little light there was hurt my eyes and I had difficulty in focusing on the black-clad figure standing with arms outstretched, framed by the rotting wood of the doorway. Her voice was sharp and icy as she ordered me to get out of the shed and go straight to the dormitory without supper. I moved as quickly as I could across the yard, through the assembly hall and up the stairs.

It was quiet, all the other boys were in their beds and the lights had been turned off. Heavy black roller blinds covered the windows ensuring that no light penetrated the vast room containing sixty beds. Twelve in each row, head to foot. A big statue of the Sacred Heart stood imposingly in one corner, the red light at his feet casting an eerie shadow onto the ceiling. I began to undress. I removed my heavy black boots and placed them carefully beneath the bed, taking care not to bang them off the chamber pot. I folded the rest of my clothes and left them at the foot of my bed.

Because of the soreness of my body and hunger, I had great difficulty in getting to sleep, constantly moving in an attempt to find a comfortable position. Just as I was about to fall asleep I heard Mother Paul's voice beside my bed asking if I had said my night prayers. When I replied that I had not, she immediately ordered me out of bed to kneel on the bare floor with my hands joined. I was not allowed to lean against the bed for support. My flimsy, striped night-shirt was a poor barrier against the cold. I said the prayer I had been taught since the day I arrived in St Michael's:

> 'Now I lay me down to sleep,
> I pray the Lord, my soul to keep,
> If I should die before I wake,
> I pray the Lord, my soul to take.
> God bless the nuns who are so good to me.'

I blessed myself and got back into bed.

It was the practice each night in St Michael's Industrial School for a nun to walk around the dormitory at eleven o'clock, ringing a large brass bell. The purpose was to awaken the boys and get them out of bed to sit on white enamelled chamber pots. We hunched on the floorboards urging our bladders or bowels to act so that we could return to bed. Many children used to fall asleep, others neglected to position their penises properly, and urinated over the rim, sending a stream of water along the floor. I liked to create a well between my legs by pressing my thighs tightly together thus allowing the urine to gather. It was a warm pleasurable feeling. Any child who wet the floor or whose nightshirt became damp received a clatter on the face from the patrolling nun as she checked those of us who had finished and held our pots for her to examine the contents. Often boys cried, as they pushed and strained to 'do' something.

One night the boy in the bed next to mine screamed, and each time he did he was slapped on the bare backside by one of the two nuns attending to him. I turned my head slowly. A ball of blood hung from his anus like a half-inflated scarlet balloon. He screamed as the nuns took it in turn to attempt to push it back up inside his body. Once he had been taken care of he was told he would be punished for what he had done. It was 'only a prolapsed bowel', Mother Paul said, as she returned to her own room. I was so terrified by the experience that the unfamiliar words stuck in my mind.

CHAPTER TWO

The children in St Michael's were divided into two groups, those between six and ten and children under six years of age. I was just over six and so I was regarded as one of the 'big boys'. As such, I was given charge of a younger child. My 'charge' was a small curly-headed blond boy I knew only as Eugene. The day he was put into my 'care' Mother Paul told me that I must take good care of him, see that he went to the toilet when he wanted to and ensure that he was kept clean, especially before and after meals. Eugene latched onto me and annoyed me by following me constantly but if I said anything to him he would start crying. I did everything I could to stop him and he was cute enough to know that I wouldn't want any of the nuns to hear him cry. One day while we were all out in the yard I left Eugene alone to play with a group of boys of my own age. I liked to play priests and altar boys and I treated the game as though it were an actual religious ceremony. I always regarded it as good training for the day I would become a priest. Halfway through the game Eugene's voice rang in my ears. So did Mother Paul's. I ran to where the child stood. A circle of children had gathered around him. I broke through and saw Eugene standing in a mound of his own excrement and urine. Tears ran in torrents from his pale blue eyes. He was dirty from the tops of his legs to the heels of his boots. Mother Paul screamed at me to clean him up, but before doing that I was to clean the yard. I stood looking at the child, my hand tightly pressed across my mouth to prevent myself from vomiting. My stomach heaving, I ran off to get a bucket of sawdust and a shovel. When I returned Eugene was still standing like a statue, yelling. I dug the shovel into the galvanized bucket of sawdust and scattered it at his feet. Then holding my breath, I told him to move, and when he was out of the way I scooped up the excrement and dumped it into the bucket. Then I took the child by the hand and brought him to the toilet. I had to take off his boots and socks, his jumper and shirt and finally his trousers. As he stood naked with much of his body covered in his own excrement, I vomited onto the cement floor. He became hysterical and to stop him being overheard I slapped my hand across his mouth and begged him not to scream. I cleaned him with some old papers that had been left in the toilet for that purpose. I held my nose with the fingers of one hand and rubbed off as much excrement as I could with the dry newspaper.

'Why are you holding your nose?' Eugene asked me.

'Because I don't like the smell,' I answered, gripping my nose tightly with the thumb and forefinger of my right hand.

'Why?' he asked.

'Because it stinks, that's why.'

He laughed at the emphasis on the word 'stinks'.

I went to the tap that hung from the wall to get some water to clean him. I turned its brass handle, and as I did it swayed on its length of lead piping.

I soaked an old newspaper in the freezing water and rubbed the child's body with it. His pale skin erupted in goose-pimples and his teeth chattered uncontrollably. He cried from the cold but there was nothing I could do. When I was finished, I warned him not to tell anyone that I had been sick. He said he wouldn't, but just to stress the point as best I could, I told him that if he opened his mouth I would kill him. Once he had committed himself not to tell anyone, I further warned him that if he told now, he would be lying and that lies would ensure instant death. Then when he was dead he would go to hell. He looked straight into my eyes and then asked me if the devil really had horns.

'He has,' I said positively, 'and he might come and stick them in you if you tell anyone that I was sick.' By the look on Eugene's face as I spoke, I knew he would not say a word about what happened in the toilet. He watched me as I swirled his dirty clothes around in a bucket of cold water to rinse them. When they were clean I threw the dirty water down the drain, wrung out the clothes and shook them to remove the wrinkles. As soon as he was dressed in clean clothes he ran out of the toilet, content.

The toilets in St Michael's were stark and cold. The rough cement floor matched the even rougher cement walls. Ventilation was by means of an 18-inch diameter hole in the wall with thick circular iron bars across it. We urinated against a cement wall which was flushed down every now and then via a piece of pipe with holes at intervals of about an inch. Sometimes I was given the task of washing down these stinking toilets. I had to use a hand-held deck-scrub and a bucket of water into which some Jeyes Fluid had been added. The waste closet was a large wooden bench with three holes cut out of it.

We sat, three at a time, with maybe another six waiting to take our places when we were finished. No partition separated one boy from the next. When one finished he shouted to the rest to 'have a look and see if you can see it floating down'. Whoever was sitting on the last hole was shouted off it so that we could all watch as the brown lumps of waste floated away. If two lumps happened to be racing towards the outlet at the same time it was certain there would be an argument as to who won. There were arguments about winners; 'He couldn't have done anything. Look, his face isn't even red and he didn't grunt either. Everyone grunts when they're going to the toilet.'

I walked back to the assembly hall with Eugene by the hand. Mother Michael had relieved Mother Paul and she had gathered the children around the gramophone. A record turned on its deck and the voice of John McCormack filled the hall. 'Machusla, Machusla, your sweet voice is calling, calling me softly . . .'

'Where were you?' Mother Michael demanded to know. 'I was in the toilet . . . cleaning my charge,' I answered.

'I hope he is properly cleaned and that his clothes are washed?' She took Eugene from me and sent him to the front of the group of children with the instruction that he listen to the music, then she told me to take a message across to the convent.

'Give it to Mother Ita,' she said, handing me a small parcel, 'and come straight back. Her bell is three rings,' she said, before remarking that I should know it anyway. I did know. Groups of us often played games guessing what different nuns' 'bells' were. Before leaving the assembly hall I had to remove my heavy black boots and put on a pair of white-soled canvas shoes.

Even though it was a part of the same building, the area of St Michael's where the nuns resided was totally different to that where we lived. The corridor leading to the convent smelled of wax from the polished floor and from the candles that burned in their holders at the feet of the statues that stood stoically against the dark wood panelled walls. My light shoes squeaked as I walked along the parquet floor. I tried to lighten my step by walking on my toes, fearful of breaking the silence. I stopped and looked out of one of the windows at the well-kept gardens, a large circular flowerbed covered with a variety of flowers swayed gently in the breeze. From the centre of this magnificent display rose a large grey-painted cross and high in the air a crucified Christ, the dead custodian of St Michael's and of the world. I gazed at this pathetic figure, his head hanging to one side crowned with thorns, his face spattered with blood, painted in bright red on sunken cheeks. His emaciated body was held to the cross by three nails that were inadequate to support the weight as it leaned slightly forward. Birds flew above the statue landing on the crown of thorns or on the outstretched arms, carelessly chattering as they did so. A robin landed and I remembered the story told so often by the nuns of how this tiny creature came to have a red breast; he was trying to pluck the thorns from the head of Christ at the time of his Crucifixion.

The corridor became narrow and much darker. A flickering light was given off from a candle burning at the feet of a large statue of the Virgin Mary. I looked around for a bell but could see none. A round brass gong hung from a silver chain and to one side there was a stick with a padded leather-bound head. I picked it up and banged the gong once, twice, then a third and final time.

I had hardly replaced the stick when a nun rushed towards me. She placed her hands on the gong to stop its sound reverberating through the convent.

'I have this message for Mother Ita,' I said, handing over the package which I had been given.

'I am Mother Ita,' she replied, her breath quickening and her voice beginning to rise.

'Who told you to ring the gong, you stupid child?'

'Mother Michael said that your bell was three.'

'It is, it is, but my God, child, do you not know the difference yet between a bell and a gong?'

I remained silent. She grabbed me by the arm, led me across the corridor to where an ornate piece of rope hung through a small hole in the ceiling, and held the tasselled end of the rope close to my face.

'This, you stupid child . . . is a bell!'

'Yes, Mother,' I answered.

'That over there,' she said turning, 'is a gong.'

Then she pointed to a small printed sign on the wall and asked me to read it.

'Bell,' I said.

'Yes, B.E.L.L.,' and with the back of her hand she slapped me across the face. 'That gong is an ornament and it is not meant to be rung, you have disturbed Jesus in the Tabernacle. The very least you could do is go to the chapel and say that you are sorry.'

The chapel was small and dimly lit by a stained-glass window depicting a cross. On either side of this there were two other smaller windows on which the black roller blinds were pulled down. The flame from the ever-burning sanctuary lamp which hung from the ceiling on its triangular chain hardly moved in the still air. The big statues made the chapel look smaller than it actually was. St Michael the Archangel, triumphant, his foot firmly placed on the back of a serpent. A snake, once the most beautiful saint in Heaven banished to eternal damnation for the sin of pride. Lucifer, serpent, symbol of evil, the devil. Out of the corner of my eye I could see the nun was watching me, and to give the impression that I was praying I bowed my head and moved my lips, certain that she would be impressed. After some minutes I found that I was actually praying.

'Lord, if it be your holy will, please don't let me get into trouble.' I was always taught that it would be wrong to ask God for anything without first prefacing the request with the words 'if it be your holy will'. Mother Ita got up from where she was kneeling but I remained in prayer just to reassure her that I was serious about what I was doing. As we left the chapel I noticed she had calmed a great deal. She ran her fingers through my hair and asked me if I was one of the new altar boys.

'Yes, Mother,' I replied.

'What age are you?' she enquired.

'Six and a little bit,' I replied confidentially.

'Well,' she said, 'didn't Jesus Himself make the odd mistake, I'm sure He'll see His way to forgiving you.

'You can tell Mother Michael that there is no message.'

I walked quickly, and on my way back to the assembly hall stopped again to look out at the figure nailed to the Cross, with a sparrow now perched on one of the outstretched arms, resting.

Twice each week we went for long walks along the country roads outside St Michael's. Before leaving we were instructed on the need to be clean, and how to behave when we were out. To salute a priest, if we met one, by raising one hand to our forehead and bringing it down sharply to our side, just as a soldier would in the army. The walk we took happened to be the same one as the priests took to say their offices from thick, black, leather-bound missals, with page-edges gilted in gold.

Lined up two-abreast, we were inspected by Mother Paul and Mother Michael. Trailing bootlaces had to be tied properly. Hair not properly combed was fixed with the black combs each of the nuns carried. I hated having my hair done by them, their strokes were heavy and the teeth hurt my scalp. When I tried to shift away from either of the nuns they gripped my chin tightly so that I could not move.

Snotty noses were wiped with checkered handkerchiefs to mutterings of 'dirty little pup'. I tried to find a place midway down the line for these walks to avoid being constantly under the eye of the leading nun, or the one at the end of the procession. This allowed a certain amount of freedom to chat with some of the other boys, and at the same time for a degree of alertness in case either of the nuns checked the line during the walk.

The large grey wooden gates swung open and enthusiastically we filed out. Talking was strictly forbidden unless we were told that it was all right. The walk was always the same, about a mile and a half out along the road and if the weather was fine we would stop in one of the many fields in the area for twenty minutes or half an hour. During this time we were allowed to break into groups and chat to each other. If the weather was not to the liking of the nuns we turned around and went back to Saint Michael's. I loved the freedom of the open fields. I picked buttercups and held them under other boys' chins to see if they were brave or cowardly. A bright yellow reflection from the skin was a sure sign of bravery, less bright the mark of a coward.

On those rare occasions when they were so engrossed in conversation that they took little notice of us, we used to sneak across the field near to a derelict house. It was a bungalow, with the path which at one time had led to its door now covered with grass and weeds. All of its windows were broken and the frames hung precariously outward. The roof was in poor condition. The slates from the apex had slid down and broken through the rusty iron guttering. Some of the others and I used to gather stones and when we got the chance we'd throw them at the roof where they landed with a sharp clack. I would turn quickly towards the nuns, watching them as they tried to discover what the noise was. I believed that the house was haunted and a banshee lived in it. Every time a stone struck the roof I ran, terrified that the banshee would appear.

Just like the other boys I was sure there was a huge hole in the floor of the house, and that any children caught would be thrown into it. Every time I got anywhere near this house I was filled with feelings of terror and a peculiar sense of delight. The fun ended with the call to 'line up'. Two by two we marched back to St Michael's and confinement.

There were days when the strict regime of the school was less in evidence. First Communion day was one. On 29 May 1957, a few months after my sixth birthday, the day before I made my first communion, I was marched to the bathroom with eight other boys. Before any of us were stripped for a bath we had to have our heads treated for lice, whether we had any or not. The lotion used was like urine to look at and had a very strong smell. It stung as it trickled down my forehead and into my eyes. I clenched them shut as I groped for something to wipe them with. Once my hair had been soaked in this foul-smelling liquid I was stripped and ordered into the bath. The heavy hand of a nun rubbed the rough flannel over my body, nudging me to lift my arms so that she could wash beneath them. Then I had to stand up, the water reaching just halfway up my shins. Naked, cold and embarrassed, I let the rest of my body be scrubbed. Mother Paul said it was important that I be 'spick and span' before Jesus entered my body.

In the bathroom there were two cast-iron baths stained from the constant dripping of water and chipped-off enamel from use over many years. It was a big room with black and red quarry tiles on the floor and dark green painted walls. There was no heating. Every second Saturday as many as sixty children waited their turn to be washed. Everyone stripped at the same time. As one child got out of the bath so another stepped into the ever clouding dirty water. Each

35

child had to dry himself and it was not unusual to have three or four boys waiting for the same towel, their bodies shivering as the carbolic-stained water ran down their bodies onto the cold floor.

I was nervous from the moment I entered the confession box to make my first confession, afraid that I would say something wrong.

'Yes?' a gruff voice said.

I took a deep breath and began: 'Bless me, Father, for I have sinned. This is my first confession, Father. Father, I told lies, Father, I was disobedient, for these and all the sins of my life I humbly ask pardon of God.'

I was not actually aware of having told lies or of having been disobedient but these were the words I had been taught in the weeks leading up to my confession. Then on the day, I recited them like a poem I had learned at school. The priest began his absolution prayer while I said an Act of Contrition. His mumbling distracted me and I lost my way halfway into the prayer I had rehearsed so often. He didn't notice, and if he did, he didn't seem to care.

On the morning of my First Communion I was not allowed to eat or drink anything. Mother Paul came into the dormitory, her arms laden with clothes. Jumpers, shirts, dicky-bows and ties as well as trousers and jackets. She tried various outfits on me before deciding that a coarse grey wool suit would look best. Instead of the usual heavy boots I was given a pair of shiny black shoes and knee-length white socks to wear. She put her two fingers into a jar of Brylcream and rubbed it into my hair before parting it at one side and then warning me not to touch it. From that moment on I was to prepare for Jesus by praying and asking him to make me worthy to receive him. Before leaving for the church I was reminded that He only stayed in my soul for fifteen minutes. It was important, during those minutes, that I prayed for anything I wanted. The importance of praying for those who looked after me was stressed. Then there were those who had died and gone to God, those that were in Purgatory. I had to pray for the souls who had gone to Limbo, babies who died before they were baptized, and who would never see God. She impressed on me the importance of praying for those who had gone to Hell because they had not led good lives. Protestants too needed prayer so that they would believe in the Blessed Virgin.

On no account was I to touch the Sacred Host with my teeth. Great care was to be exercised to ensure that the host did not fall out of my mouth and even if it did I was never to touch it with my hands. Only the priest could do that. If it became stuck on the roof of my mouth it was permissible for me to gently peel it away using my tongue.

Having gone to the altar-rails and taken the white host into my mouth I returned solemnly to my seat where I bowed my head and closed my eyes. My prayers were a sort of a test for Jesus. I never did pray for the nuns. Nor did I pray for the souls of those who had died in a state of sin and, as for Protestants, I never mentioned them. I was very specific about what I wanted. I asked Him to bring me an apple and an orange and sixpence. I had seen apples and oranges but never tasted either. Despite the fervour of my prayer, the fruits never materialized and I only got half the money I asked for.

Later in the day, Miss Sharpe, our singing teacher, brought us out for a walk through the town. It was a hot sunny day and the local people who were standing at their hall doors stared at us. Groups of local children laughed and jeered, mocking our clothes. Some of the older people gave us money. I got a thrupenny bit and, if I could manage to hide it, I was going to buy three ice-pops. Miss Sharpe went into a shop and bought a bag of sweets while we waited outside gaping through the window. We walked until we came to a field where she suggested we go in and sit down. She sat on the grass for a while and then moved to where there was a big grey boulder. She sat up on it and called us to gather round her so that she could share out the sweets. Before doing that she asked had any of us got any money, I admitted that I had and she took it from me saying that it was part payment for the sweets. We were not allowed to have money. She gave us two sweets each and said that she would raffle the remainder before we went home. Just as St Michael's was home for us so it was for her. We gathered daisies and made them into a long chain, looping one through the pinched-out stem of the other. I pulled some grass from the field and tossed it into the air, explaining to one of the other boys that this was how farmers tested to see which way the wind was blowing.

I lay on the grass propped up with my hand under my chin and my elbow dug firmly into the ground. My eyes shifted in the direction of Miss Sharpe. I noticed her sandaled feet and as I looked up along her leg I could see where her stocking-top was gathered and held by a suspender. Her bare thigh was pure white in contrast with the tan colour of the stocking and the pale yellow colour of her knickers which were elasticated firmly higher up her leg. I wanted to tell one of the other boys but I decided against it, just in case he told on me. I watched for as long as I thought it was safe to, enjoying the sensations that rippled through my body. Something inside suggested that the pleasure I was getting from watching this lady was sinful, but that didn't matter. The feeling of pleasure outweighed everything.

Eventually I got up and went over to a part of the field where some of the boys had gathered. Our supervisor did not seem to mind. In a hole in a stone wall we could hear the buzzing of what we presumed to be a hive of bees or wasps, nobody knew the difference. I couldn't resist the temptation to poke a long piece of stick into the hole. As I probed around the buzzing intensified and, too late, one of the boys warned me that they would emerge and sting the life out of us.

The insects streamed from the hole and we all ran, pursued by them. Agitated wasps bent on revenge stung most of us, and as they did we screamed. My own face and legs were sore and I found it difficult to run as Miss Sharpe ushered us from the field, her headscarf tied tightly about her face.

Curious villagers watched as we were walked back down the town, each of us holding a different part of our bodies.

'What happened to the poor children?' an old lady asked.

'Wasps,' Miss Sharpe replied acidly, 'they got stung.'

'Ah sure God help them.'

'Indeed,' Miss Sharpe said, 'God help them.'

One by one, stung and weeping we walked through the gates of St Michael's. Hearing us, Mother Paul rushed out and demanded to know what all the commotion was about. Miss Sharpe told her what happened.

'Well now,' the nun intoned, 'we all know that wasps and bees don't sting for nothing, and we all know, don't we, that some little devil has to disturb them? Is anyone going to own up?' she said as she swung her pointed finger round the group of us. No-one spoke. She waited, then reminded us that it was not long since Jesus came to visit us.

'It's as well to be aware,' she continued, 'that He knows.' She ordered us to the dispensary, saying that whatever pain or suffering we were enduring was entirely of our own making. We would have to put up with it until she was ready to attend to us.

The dispensary was a small room where any cuts or

grazes were dressed, usually with iodine and a big lump of cotton wool held in position with a piece of sticking plaster. It was a dark room, with many presses, all of which had glass doors. On the shelves inside, bottles of different colours and shapes were carefully labelled and fitted with cork stoppers. Cotton wool was wrapped in purple paper, its whiteness contrasting sharply with the colour of its wrapper. The air smelled heavily of disinfectant.

As we sat and waited on the wooden benches I warned the others not to say a word. The doors were flung open and Mother Paul rushed in to attend to us. As she dabbed iodine onto the various stings she said she hoped that there was no-one telling lies. Nobody was. Nobody was saying anything. I felt a great sense of relief as I left the room, my stings had been anointed and I was not found out. As I walked down the short passage which would bring me to the school yard Mother Paul shouted after me to tell the other boys that they were to take off their communion clothes, fold them, and leave them ready for her to collect. I was glad to get out of the coarse wool suit as the rough hems on the trousers had scorched my legs, and the jacket felt heavy across my shoulders. Communion day was over.

CHAPTER THREE

Much of the time in St Michael's was given to training us to be altar boys and to serve Mass in the local parish church. I often spent three or four hours a day learning the Latin responses. A small fat nun gave out the responses in a monotonous voice and made me repeat them. Another hour was set aside for the practice of the ritualistic movements necessary on the altar during Mass. I learned the foreign words without the least understanding of what they meant. I knelt, stood, bowed, joined my hands while the nun played the role of priest. I learned to move the large missal and brass stand from one side of the altar to the other at the right moment and at the right speed. Reverence for the blessed sacrament was everything. I was constantly reminded of the need to keep my hands clean and my hair combed. My hands would not just be carrying cruets of wine or a chalice full of white hosts. The wine would become the blood of Christ and the hosts his body. When I was not moving sacred items I had to kneel absolutely still, with my hands joined and my eyes fixed on the crucified Christ just over the tabernacle. Being an altar boy gave me a sense of importance. I loved it, loved the stillness of early morning in the town. The sun shone low in the eastern sky, slanting its way across dark slated roofs and onto the narrow streets of Cappoquin. As I started my walk the streets were silent except for the sound of my hobnailed boots click-clacking on the pavement. The neat rows of houses looked as though nobody lived in them, their curtains still drawn. As I neared the church, which was about ten minutes walk from the Industrial School, people opened their hall doors to check the weather or to sweep the dust from the pavement in front of their houses. Some greeted me, others didn't say anything and I often felt that they were trying to avoid me. I used to hear people refer to me as 'one of the children from the orphanage', which was the phrase locals used to soften the brutal reality of the industrial school in their midst.

The church was on a hill overlooking the town. It was surrounded by black railings that always had the appearance of being newly painted. Moist, glistening cobwebs had formed between the rails during the night and I loved to cup my hand and scoop them off, trying not to damage them as I did. I examined the cobwebs closely to see what had been trapped there. There were small flies and midges, dead or dying. Breakfast for a hungry spider was ruined many a time due to my clumsy efforts at replacing the web between the rails from which I had taken it. My attempts at delicacy could not match those of the original spinner of the beautiful silken webs.

The sacristy was at the back of the church and the first thing I had to do on entering it was bless myself and then remove my heavy boots and replace them with soft plimsoll runners. My soutane and surplice were in a cupboard, ironed and starched, ready for me to wear. If there was time before or between Masses the sacristan would allow the altar boys out into the church yard for a game of handball, always stressing the importance of keeping clean and tidy. Playing with a ball in a snow white surplice was difficult, there was always the risk of getting it dirty from a hopping ball or a fall. If that happened an angry sacristan would forbid the serving of Mass. Since that was a risk I was not prepared to take I very seldom played handball.

The priest robed for Mass, constantly praying as he put on each vestment. The amice, the alb, the cincture, the stole, and the chasuble, each with its own significance and its own prayer. If he wanted assistance it was always given to him. Some priests preferred to robe without help.

I stood at the sacristy door looking into the darkened church slowly filling with morning worshippers. They genuflected in the centre of the church and then men and women went to their respective sides of the centre aisle. The women wore head scarves. The men took off their hats or caps as they entered the church. The sacristan put on some lights, the brown bakelite switches clicking loudly in the silence, then he struck a match and lit the white taper wick fitted to the top of a smooth dark brown wooden pole. Slowly and solemnly I walked out of the sacristy and ascended the red carpeted steps to light the three candles on either side of the altar. The congregation moved and even though I had my back to them, I could feel their eyes on me.

In the sacristy the priest waited for the altar boys to lead him onto the altar. His hands were joined tightly and his index fingers pressed hard against his well-shaven chin. His eyes were lowered and his head bowed. Priests, once vested, seldom spoke, and when they did it was usually to say that something was wrong.

The congregation rose to its feet as every light was switched on, the brightest ones being over the altar. If it was an 'Ordinary Mass' there would be only two altar boys serving, and as I was normally on the right hand side of the priest, I would be more involved in the ritual than the other boy. I had to move the missal, ring the bells at the offertory and communion, sound the gong at the consecration and hold the paten under the chins of the people receiving communion. It was a role I thoroughly enjoyed. I always felt as though I was on a stage performing for an audience. I knew that there would be a nun from the school there, they always attended the Masses being served by any of 'their children'.

One morning, when Mass was over, I disrobed, taking great care about how I hung my soutane and surplice. Walking down the town I noticed Mother Paul ahead of me and deliberately slowed my pace so as not to catch up with her. Some people were polishing the brass fittings on their front doors, and as the day threatened to be hot and sunny, they covered their 'scumbled' or painted hall doors in colourful canvas sheets with holes for the bell, knocker and doorknob to protrude. I heard men and women comment on how the sun caused the paint to blister.

As I neared St Michael's, I noticed Mother Paul standing, beckoning me to hurry. I was gripped with fear as I quickened my step. Thoughts of what I could have done now ran through my mind. Once I had caught up with her, she told me to walk in front of her.

'You were very good on the altar this morning. I am going to suggest to the sacristan that you be allowed to do more altar boy duties in future. You can be a very good child when you want to be.'

I walked ahead, smiling to myself. It was the first time she had ever praised me for anything. I was just six and a half when I began serving Mass. The ease with which I mastered Latin was a topic of conversation among nuns and priests. Altar boys were highly regarded in the community. I was proud of myself and delighted in being referred to as the 'little altar boy'.

I was thin and often jeered at by other children. Those from the town were the worst offenders, referring to me as 'a skinny little orphan'. The jeering hurt and I was often close to tears. That would have suited my tormentors but I was not prepared to give in to them.

Sunday was my favourite day for serving. Flowers adorned the altar in brass vases and many more candles burned than for weekday Masses. The crowd was bigger and the organ droned constantly in the background. The sound of the choir singing filled the church and added to the pomp of the occasion. Instead of the usual black and white, the altar boys wore bright red soutanes and well-starched pure white surplices. The priest's vestments were also more colourful than usual. A white chasuble with a golden cross embroidered on the back and the scripted letters I.H.S. in the centre.

Before Mass, the priest spent a great deal of time going through the big red missal from which he would read. The chosen sections were marked, each with a different coloured ribbon. A final check through it and he nodded to the sacristan indicating that the book could be placed on the heavy brass stand and brought to the altar. He carried it and as he placed it on the right hand side of the altar he checked that all candles had been lit. On this religious stage everything had to be correct.

Once I reached the altar there was tension and drama. There was the fear of forgetting a line, a response, the thought that a wine cruet might slip from my hand. My heart raced as I rang the bell to warn the congregation of the approaching consecration, that part of the Mass when white host and red wine became the body and blood of

Jesus Christ. Transubstantiation. The silence was palpable. I struck the brass domed gong firmly: Bong. Heads down. Bong. The white host held aloft as the bowed heads looked up momentarily, in adoration. Bong, eyes and heads lowered again. Now the priest prayed over the chalice of wine. Bong, he genuflected, Bong, each head rose and gave praise to the gold cup containing the blood of Jesus Christ. A final bong and the solemnity and tension of the Consecration gave way to a restless shifting of bodies, clearing of throats, and the distinctive sound of people blowing their noses.

Before the distribution of Communion two altar boys draped stiffly-starched cloths over the marble top of the altar rails. The bell sounded, indicating to people that it was time to approach the altar rails. Men and women left their seats on the different sides of the church and took their places on either side of the centre gate leading onto the altar. Men on the right, women on the left. I often carried the gold paten which I held under the chins of those receiving Communion, in case the host fell. As I walked carefully backwards with the priest, I couldn't help noticing the various ways people offered their tongues to receive the host. The men seemed to be in a hurry and opened their mouths rapidly, unleashing their tongues on the white host like a lizard whipping up its prey. Their tongues were dirty, yellow tobacco-stained and rough in appearance. Women were much less hurried and more reverent in their approach. There was a sensuality about the way they parted their lips and put out their tongues. They usually left the altar rails slowly, walking on the toes of their shoes, so as not to break the silence with their stiletto heels. The men were heavy footed.

Hands joined, heads bowed, the entire congregation spent the next fifteen minutes in silent prayer, each undoubtedly requesting a different favour from the Visitor now within their bodies.

Every weekday after serving Mass I had to call into the local post office to collect any letters or parcels there might be for the Industrial School. It was a quaint old building serving the townspeople as a newsagents, a hardware store and a confectioners. The exterior was painted dark green with the words 'Oifig an Phoist' beautifully written in gold lettering over the entrance. There was a gold harp at the beginning and end of the hand-painted sign. The window display consisted of some faded cigarette packets, magazines and newspapers, discoloured by the sun. The entrance was through a double-sided door, one side of which was always open. When the breadman came it was necessary to open both sides, or when the sacks of mail were very bulky. I had to wait as the postman and the shop owner sorted through the letters, stacking them according to the particular area of the town they were going to. Each batch was then put into sacks with the letters P&T imprinted on them in heavy black printing ink. The local postman became a particular friend to me. He was a small, chubby man, always smiling, chatting, or singing. Whenever he saw me he'd say, 'How's me man this morning then?' before remarking to the other people in the shop that one day I would be the best postman the town had ever seen. When he asked me if I was going to be a postman when I grew up, I said I wasn't. I was going to be a priest.

'A priest, begob,' he replied. 'Well I suppose you could do worse.'

He used to take me by the hand and bring me over to the counter where the cakes were, eclairs with chocolate, tarts with jam seeping through their crusty sides, fairy cakes and currant buns.

'What'll ye have?' he would ask.

After spending some time scanning the wooden trays I would normally settle for a currant cake covered in sugar. The postman paid for it and I'd sit down to eat it while he packed the bag that I was to carry. He told me not to leave a trace of it as he didn't want 'them nuns' coming up the road after him.

'I've nothing against nuns, son, I love them really, at a distance.' He roared laughing.

I always felt uneasy sitting there eating cakes and I used to stuff them into my mouth as quickly as I could, afraid that some of the local people might mention to the nuns that they had seen me. There was no doubt in my mind as to what the consequences of that would be. The postman insisted that I carry the post like a 'real postman'. 'Over yer shoulder, that way it won't feel so heavy.' I did as he instructed and when I was ready to leave he'd clap his hands together before saying, 'Right now, begob, you're away with it.'

Instead of going back into the school I would have to go to the convent door and hand in the bag containing letters and parcels. It was a big oak door, with very ornate and well-maintained brass fittings. The bellpush was set into a circular brass disc with the words 'press' etched into its white convex-shaped button. I pressed it and waited. I heard the lock being opened and prepared to hand over the bag. The nun that took the post from me never spoke to me nor I to her. She closed the door and I walked the few yards further on to the grey gates leading into the yard of St Michael's. As I crossed the yard I could hear the sound of mugs and plates being collected through the large open windows. After a few minutes silence the collective voices of the other children chanted grace after meals.

After delivering the post one Friday morning, I knocked on the kitchen door. A fat, small, wrinkled-faced nun opened it and glowered at me. I told her I had been answering Mass and that I had missed breakfast. My excuse was a good one. I would get my porridge, my dripping-covered bread and a mug of cocoa.

'Wait,' she snapped as she let the door slam. I stood, looking around the large grey dining room, for the first time noticing how big it really was. Everyone was gone, the tables were cleared. In the distance I could hear the other children playing. The kitchen door swung open and a tin plate of porridge was pushed into my hands.

'Leave it at one of the tables and come back for cocoa and bread.'

I did as instructed. The porridge was cold and very lumpy, the bread greasy and the cocoa had a skin on its surface. As I ate, the sweating nun emerged from the kitchen carrying a brown bottle, from which she poured a thick dark liquid. She tossed a tablespoon of syrup of figs into my mouth.

'Lick that spoon clean and swallow,' she demanded. I hated the stuff and made no secret of that. I used to hold it in my mouth hoping the nun would go away so that I could spit it out. She stayed, watching, until my mouth was empty. Everyone got a spoonful of syrup of figs once a week. As I was washing my mug and plate she asked me to take a message up the town for her. She didn't wait for an answer, just rushed back into the kitchen and emerged a few moments later carrying a canework basket, with a live chicken inside.

'You know where the other convent is?' she asked.

'Yes.' I hesitated before adding, 'Mother.' My eyes were riveted on the basket. She held it up for me to take from her and when I didn't take it immediately she left it on the floor.

The top was held closed with two leather straps and buckles. The chicken poked its head out through a grille on one side. Then it began to flutter about, frightened. I lifted the basket, holding the grille section towards my legs, thus allowing the chicken to take a peck at me. I jumped, and quickly turned it the other way round.

'Give that message to Mother Immaculate,' she said.

I walked out of the dining hall, through the assembly hall into the yard where I was immediately surrounded by inquisitive children.

'What's in the basket? Where are you going?' Some laughed at the difficulty I was having in holding the basket steady. It was heavy and I had to stop repeatedly in order to change it from one hand to the other.

The street near the school was quiet, and the houses on each side of it basked in the sun. At one of the houses two old men leaned over their half-door, both smoking pipes and wearing hats. They took it in turns to spit out onto the street or greet people going by. I had often heard the older boys talk about these men. They were brothers, known as the two Toms. Tom Dee and Tom Tee. I had heard more than once that they had a big hole in the floor just inside the door of their house and that one of their 'tricks' was to try and lure children in, so they would fall into it. Once dead, the children were fed to the greyhounds they kept in the backyard. I believed the story and shivered as I walked by, even though I was on the opposite side of the street. Out of the corner of my eye I watched, just in case one of them chased me.

An inquisitive dog sniffed at the basket. As he barked the bird became frightened and fluttered furiously. I was still terrified of dogs.

'Go away,' I said.

My heartbeat quickened and my breath became uneven

and hurried. I became very frightened. The barking dog attracted more dogs and as they followed me I began to run. They ran too, snapping at the chicken. I held the basket high in the air and screamed. Some of the dogs jumped, bared their teeth and growled viciously again. People rushed to their front doors, some said that none of the dogs would bite, others told me to stop running. One man tried to stop me by saying that it was the chicken they were after. Nothing they said eased my fear. I continued running.

Ahead of me I could see the green gate leading into the convent. When I reached it I grabbed the latch and quickly pushed the gate open. I kicked out at the dogs to get them away from me before banging the gate shut. I stood with my back to the wooden gate listening to the barking animals. I was perspiring heavily and as I looked at the basket now lying on the gravel path I began to cry uncontrollably, sobbing hysterically, fighting for each breath.

I badly needed to go to the toilet. I undid the braces holding the buttons at the back of my trousers. In this hunched position, I defecated on the gravel. There was never toilet paper supplied in the school, but out there in the open I instinctively wanted to wipe my backside and looked around for something I could use, there was nothing. I pulled my trousers back on and stuffed my shirt inside them before using my foot to shift some stones into a pile to cover the stool. Just as I was finishing off the gravel mound I heard footsteps coming towards me from around a bend on the walkway to the convent.

I grabbed the basket and took a quick glance at the pile of stones, pressed lightly on it with my foot, picked up the basket, and was just about to move off when a tall nun asked me what I was doing.

'It's a message for Mother Immaculate,' I answered nervously.

'I am Mother Immaculate,' she said and reached out to take the basket. It was then she noticed the pile of stones.

'What is this?' she said, pointing. I told her about being chased by the dogs, that I was tired, and had sat down to play with the stones. Then she asked me to leave the basket down, before walking towards the heaped stones.

She kicked them. I watched as her shoe became embedded in the mixture of gravel and excrement. Her anger at me was obvious from the expression on her face.

'You filthy dirty little pup,' she said, 'you will be severely punished for this.'

I tried to speak but she wouldn't allow me to. I wanted to explain how frightened I had been, and how I couldn't help doing what I had done, but she wouldn't listen. I offered an apology but she ignored me.

She rushed over to a patch of grass and dragged her shoe back and forth through it trying to clean it. 'You will pay for this, you dirty brat. As sure as there is a God in Heaven, you'll pay for this.' The idea of running did occur to me but I realized that such a move would make my situation worse. Mother Immaculate strode forward and grabbed me by the ear lobe.

'If I had a dog's lead I'd put it around your neck,' she said, 'because it's only dogs that do what you have done.'

The basket remained on the ground as she opened the gate, and began walking me back down the town while holding me by the ear.

Inside St Michael's I was pushed towards the part of the yard where Mother Paul was sitting.

'What has the pup done now, Mother Immaculate?' she enquired.

The two nuns discussed what had happened and I could

52

see Mother Paul become more and more annoyed. They both looked down at Mother Immaculate's shoe and then at me. Mother Paul grabbed me as the other nun left.

'Why didn't you go to the toilet before you left?' she asked.

'Because I didn't want to, Mother,' I answered.

'But you should have gone,' she yelled, as she hit me across the face, 'instead of behaving like a wild animal.'

I remained silent. I saw the cane slide down from under her sleeve and it swished across my legs.

'That hurts,' I shouted.

'It will hurt a lot more I promise before I'm finished with you. You're no better than a dog.' She hit me with the cane again before ordering me to go to the dormitory and wait for her. As I walked away from her she shouted, 'You should be ashamed of yourself, an altar boy. You're a disgrace. And you better start walking properly or you'll get more of this cane than you bargained for.' Nothing had ever been said to me before about my manner of walking. I bowed my head and watched my feet. I could see nothing wrong, yet somehow I had become conscious of every step I was taking, and was aware that unless I changed the way I walked, Mother Paul would be even more severe in her punishment of me.

As I slowly made my way up the long wooden stairs to the dormitory I was followed by another boy.

'Mother Paul said you're not to lie on your bed, or sit on it. You're to stand beside it until she has time to deal with you.'

The dormitory was cold and dark even though the sun was shining. I stood by my bed as I had been told, too frightened to do anything else. From the dining room, I could smell food and hear the sounds of the other boys having dinner. I was hungry. When dinner was finished I could hear them playing 'tig'. I knew that others would be playing priests and altar boys. I wondered who was acting as priest, since it was usually me who played that role.

I began to cry remembering the last time I had been beaten, the stinging of the cane and the nun's taunting as she delighted in my terror. Without warning the image returned of a man's body trembling violently as it hung from a short length of rope tied to an alder tree. It became so real that I was certain I could touch it. I shifted uneasily from one foot to the other, trying desperately to block out the vision. I trembled violently and then screamed, a high-pitched, piercing cry that echoed through the stillness of the dormitory down to the assembly hall. As I yelled at the image to 'get away', Mother Paul grabbed me tightly by the shoulders and slapped me across the face.

'What in the name of God,' she shouted, 'is the matter with you?'

'I saw the man hanging.'

'What man?' she asked.

'I don't know, Mother, just a man.'

She hit me again. 'This nonsense will have to stop, it's distressing the other children. What you are seeing is just in your imagination. People don't hang themselves. You're here for us to look after because your parents are dead. You'll see them again when you die, provided you get to heaven and that is where they are.'

I remained silent. She told me to get undressed and prepare to take the punishment I deserved. I trembled, taking my clothes off, from both the cold and the knowl-edge of what I knew I was going to have to endure. Mother Paul walked towards the dormitory door, took a large key from the pocket of her habit and locked it. I hadn't finished undressing by the time she returned to my bedside. She became agitated and shouted at me to hurry.

'The sooner we get this over,' she said, 'the sooner I can be getting on with my work.'

Once undressed, I lay on my side. Mother Paul told me to lie face down. I noticed a tremor in her voice, a nervous excitement.

'I'm only going to give you a light spanking,' she said, 'as long as you promise not to tell anyone I let you off with the punishment you should be getting.'

I didn't answer her. I tensed my body and waited for the cane to strike, but it didn't. Her hand slapped me gently on the bare backside, then with the other hand she rubbed the area she had just hit. I was nervous, desperately anxious, and unsure. I could hear her breath, deep and rushing through her nostrils. She ran her fingers down the centre of my back and out towards my shoulder-blades. Then she eased them along the full length of my body in long, gentle, sweeping movements.

'Lie over on your back,' she said.

I turned slowly and looked into her flushed face. She held my limp penis in her hand and drew back the foreskin. It hurt slightly but I was too frightened to say anything.

'You must make sure that you do this every time you are washing yourself, it's very important to keep that part of your body clean.' She moved the skin backwards and forwards until I had an erection. A sensation I had never experienced swept through my body causing me to squirm and writhe involuntarily. When it had passed I sobbed uncontrollably, frightened at what had happened.

She explained that what I had experienced sometimes happened to boys and men when they are washing their 'private parts' and added that it was not a sin.

'Sometimes boys and men play with themselves for pleasure. Not only is that a sin, it is a mortal sin which can only be forgiven by a Bishop in confession. It is up to him to decide whether to give absolution or not. If he doesn't, then that black stain will remain on your soul for ever. If that happened you certainly would never see your father or mother again with God in Heaven. Now get dressed, and remember, nobody is to be told I let you off so lightly.' She unlocked the dormitory door and watched as I dressed.

Downstairs, in the assembly hall, I could hear the other children playing, and when I had my clothes on I walked towards the door leading to the stairs. As I passed her, Mother Paul hit me across the back of the head with the full force of her hand and, losing my footing, I fell down the stairs. I tried to break my fall as I tumbled but could not. I landed on my back in the hall. She rushed down the stairs after me shouting, 'You filthy dirty pup.'

I got to my feet and ran.

'Stop, stop,' she screamed, 'before I have to deal with you again.' Her tenderness in the dormitory had evaporated and was now replaced by a rage I had not seen in her before. When she eventually caught me she hit me across the face and I ran away from her. She shouted at some of the other boys to catch me. One grabbed my jumper and held it until she took over.

'How many times am I going to have to ask you to stop dragging that foot after you?' She struck me again, this time on the right side of my face.

'If you don't stop dragging it then as sure as God is in Heaven, I'll ensure that you don't serve Mass again.'

The idea of not being allowed to serve Mass hurt more than the physical punishment. Walking away, I looked down at my feet and wondered what I was doing wrong.

Mother Paul brushed past me and indicated with her finger that I was to follow. She walked towards the boiler room, opened the doors and pushed me inside. I tripped and fell. She didn't wait to see if I was all right. The doors closed and I heard her putting a brush across the two handles so that I could not open them. I remained on the floor crying for a few minutes before realizing the torture was finished.

The boiler room was dark except for a weary yellow flame trying to ignite the coals which had been stacked in the grate of the black range. Through the iron bars of the door I watched the flame leaping and bobbing. Slowly the coals lit and the room warmed, I was content in the heat and happy to remain where I was for a long time. I thought of hell as I watched the coals redden and once again I wished Mother Paul would go straight there and burn.

As the heat of the fire intensified, so did the noise. An eerie howl as the hot air was drawn up the chimney. I found a piece of old newspaper on the floor and began to tear it into little pieces which I tossed into the fire. It burned quickly, before its blackened remains rose on the hot air currents and disappeared.

The peace of the boiler room was broken by the sound of the brush being removed from the door. Mother Paul pushed the doors open, allowing the colder air of the outside to sweep through the room and chill the warmth I had been so comfortable in.

She told me to go to the dining room and have my supper. When I was finished, the boots belonging to the other boys had to be polished and shone. One of the other boys would help me.

I took my place at the table, waiting for the big jug of cocoa to come around to fill my tin mug. The bread was coated in lard that stuck to the roof of my mouth as I ate it, allowing the weak, watery cocoa to take the greasy feeling from my mouth.

Like every meal, it was taken in silence. After supper as I walked out of the dining room, Mother Paul grabbed me by the arm and asked me if there was something wrong with my boots.

I told her they were a bit tight and that they were hurting my toes. They were not hurting me at all but I felt I had to offer some excuse in order to avoid further punishment.

'Go to Mr O'Rourke in the morning and see if he can do anything about them for you,' she said.

'Yes, Mother,' I replied.

When all the other boys were gone to the dormitory, John Cleary and I began the twice weekly task of polishing and shining their boots. On this occasion he did the polishing and I the shining. One by one, pair by pair, until all sixty pairs were finished. Then they had to be put into boxes on the wall, each box with its number corresponding to a tag on the back of every pair. It was a tedious and tiring process, but to relieve the boredom we chatted quietly to each other. Cleary asked why Mother Paul had called me a dirty little pup.

'Because of the big gick I did under the stones up in the other convent.'

'What gick?' he laughed.

'The one that Mother Immaculate stuck her foot in,' I said.

John laughed hysterically. 'Shut up,' I said, knowing we would get into trouble if caught laughing or talking when we were supposed to be doing something. Invariably, when we were laughing, one or other of the nuns would accuse us of laughing or jeering at them, or talking about something dirty. Once we had finished and tidied away the tins of polish and brushes, we went to bed. It was late and most of the other boys were asleep. With a fleeting 'good night' we parted, he to one end of the big room and I to the other. At the sound of a nun approaching I took my hands from under the bedcovers and folded them prayer-like across my chest. She reminded me to include in my prayers all those who were so good to me, particularly the nuns who looked after me. Because of the fear of dying that had been instilled from my first days in the school, the prayer I said most fervently each night was: 'If I should die before I wake . . .' Mother Paul frequently reminded us that we could never tell the day, or the hour, when God would call.

Mr O'Rourke was the convent handyman. He did everything from farming the few acres of land the nuns had, to weeding the flowerbeds at the front of the convent. I went looking for him to see if he could do anything about my boots. He was an elderly man with wrinkled pock-marked skin and an almost bald head on which he wore a cap with the peak to one side. He was a quiet, soft-spoken, shy man. The first place I went to look for him was the farm. In the distance I saw him leading two horses as he steered a plough. The smell of freshly-turned earth was evident. Overhead a flock of birds swooped and dived to pick the succulent worms unearthed by the plough. I stood at the edge of the field watching man and animals move in unison. I watched birds fighting over juicy worms and waved to him but he didn't notice. He was puffing contentedly at his pipe and concentrating on the furrow he was ploughing. When he eventually noticed me he took the pipe from his mouth, held it in his hand and spat onto the ploughed clay before waving back. Once finished, the horses were freed to roam an adjoining field. He walked towards me. The crests and troughs in the field exaggerated his limp, giving his body a deformed appearance. He greeted me with an affectionate toothless smile, enquiring what the nuns wanted this time.

I told him that Mother Paul had sent me to him to see if he could do anything about my boots because they were too tight.

'What I like about the ploughing is this,' he said. 'It's grand to be out there on your own with the smell of the clay. I get away from the nuns for a while and I can smoke me ould pipe without a bother. Mind now, I wouldn't say that to them, but I know you won't say a word to anyone.' He lifted his cap and wiped his head with the back of his right arm. Both of us stood there for a while looking out over the field he had just finished working on. The birds continued to land, grab at a worm and resume their flight, pursued by a more aggressive flyer anxious to have everything his way.

'Come on so, me lad, and we'll see what we can do for ye.' He led the way through the convent orchard to a greenhouse where we both sat down on a wooden bench. He told me he knew me from serving Mass in the local church.

'What's this they call ye?'

'Pat,' I answered.

'That's a great name, Patrick. That's the man they say drove all the snakes out of Ireland. Did ye know that?'

'I did,' I answered.

He asked me to give him a look at the boots. I undid the laces as he scraped out the bowl of his pipe with a penknife. I sat there in my stockinged feet watching him cut slices from a block of tobacco and then rub it delicately between his palms before pressing it into the bowl of his pipe. He struck a match and waited a few seconds, explaining to me that a pipe should never be lit while there is still sulphur on the match – 'It gives the tobacco a horrid taste.'

Slowly he sucked on the pipe and drew the flame from the match into the bowl. I could see the tobacco redden and as he released the smoke from his mouth, the greenhouse was temporarily filled in a ghostly mist. He waved his hand to disperse the smoke and picked up one of my boots. He pulled the leather in an effort to stretch it and, with his penknife, scraped at the inside, taking away tiny slivers of leather. He did the same with the second boot, and told me to put them on to see how they felt.

'They're fine,' I said. He suggested that we walk through the orchard just to be certain, and to see if there might be anything worth eating.

It was too early in the year for fruit to be ripe but that did not prevent me biting into a pear he picked from a fan-shaped tree growing against a wall bathed in sunshine.

'D'ye see them goosegogs?' Mr O'Rourke said as we passed a bush laden with green gooseberries. 'Them's the lads that'd give ye a right pain in the belly.'

I couldn't resist the temptation to take one. It was sour and I immediately spat out the piece I had bitten off. The old man laughed as I threw away what was left.

'They're a great man for to clean out the bowels, better than any bottle ye could buy.' He laughed and I laughed too, though I didn't understand what he meant. He asked I would be serving Mass the following morning and when I told him I would he pressed a multi-sided threepenny piece into my hand saying that it was for spending on the way back from church. He warned me in a good-humoured way not to let the nuns see the money. I agreed.

'I better be getting on with me work before them nuns is coming after me with the cane. Now begob that wouldn't do at all.' He laughed loudly as we went our different directions, he into the orchard and I back to the concrete yard where there was a game of football going on. A big statue of the Sacred Heart with arms outstretched looked down on the match. I gazed back at the statue and read the plaque underneath: 'Suffer little children to come unto me' with the date 1876. Then I checked my feet, trying to ensure that I was walking properly. I couldn't be certain any more.

CHAPTER FOUR

The only respite I had from the daily grind of St Michael's was when I became ill. I was about seven when I contracted measles, and on seeing the raspberry-like rash covering my body, Mother Paul immediately ordered me out of the main dormitory and into a smaller room with twelve beds, which was reserved for any of us who became ill. The 'sick bay' was cleaner and brighter than the main dormitory. Instead of bare floorboards it had a brightly patterned linoleum. The reason for the lino became obvious as more children were ill. Many of them were so bad that they vomited repeatedly onto the floor much to the annoyance of the nuns and the dislike of the boys who were not sick and had to clean it up. Being sick had advantages: the food was better. The porridge was warmer and sweeter and somehow the bread seemed fresher. Dinner was the most improved meal of all. Instead of the usual sloppy stew, anyone who was sick was given pandy; a mixture of finely mashed potato, milk and butter, with a little salt. It was served on plastic plates instead of the usual tin ones.

I lay quietly in the small dormitory listening to the sounds from the yard as the other boys played. A bell summoned them to dinner and everything was quiet. In the stillness I heard the sound of the train making its way into the station. The dark roller blinds were pulled down as protection from bright light. Mother Paul told us that bright light would be very bad for our eyes while we had measles. As I listened to the train's puffing and panting I couldn't resist going to the window and lifting one corner of the blind.

The light hurt my eyes at first, I had grown so used to the darkness, but despite that I persisted. The familiar cloud of smoke billowed into the air to be dispersed around the yard and replaced by another. The whistle sounded and the brake was applied causing the wheels to screech. The following wagons banged roughly into each other. Within minutes everything was silent as the tender filled with water in preparation for another journey. The room I was in was so close to the station and the day so still, that I could hear the driver and his mate discussing where they would go for a drink.

On the stairs I heard the dull thud of heavy boots, I knew it wasn't a nun, because of the absence of the jangle of her long rosary beads hitting off her habit as she walked, but just as a precaution I got back into bed. John Cleary came into the room carrying a tray with a plate of pandy on it. He mimicked Mother Paul as he left it down on my bed, first puckering his mouth, then squinting his eyes and, in a squeaky high-pitched voice, saying, 'I want to see every bit of that eaten, not a trace is to be left on the plate. Do you understand, child?' Before he left the room he asked me to breathe on him so that he would get the measles too.

Gradually the sick bay filled with red-faced boys; some really sick, others just with a rash. It was not usual for us to have pillows on our beds; we didn't have any in the main dormitory, and as more of us became bored just lying in bed with nothing to do, I decided on a pillow-fight. I challenged one of the boys and when he refused, stood on my bed

64

shouting, 'Coward, coward,' to provoke him. He couldn't resist swinging his pillow at me and, as I stooped to pick up mine, he hit me and knocked me onto the floor. I attempted to get back into bed while he belted me to the encouragement of the other boys. Eventually I managed to get back onto the bed and was caught up in the excitement and anger of the fight. I gripped the corners of the pillowcase firmly and dug my feet into the mattress before swinging as hard as I could. He ducked and the pillow crashed into the iron-framed head of the bed, its light cover bursting open and the feathers floating around the room. I was left holding an empty pillowcase.

Some of the boys laughed. I panicked and asked them to help me put them back. I pleaded that if they didn't I would get into awful trouble. Realizing I wasn't going to get help, I rushed around the room gathering fistfuls of feathers and stuffing them into the cover they had exploded from. Those I could not collect I blew along the floor until they were underneath the beds. Mother Paul arrived into the dormitory to enquire how we were. Nervously I told her that I was feeling a bit better before adding that I thought my pillow was torn.

'I tried to fix it,' I said, 'but some of the feathers fell out.' She looked at me suspiciously, but said nothing, took the pillow and walked out of the room. I wondered if she would bring a different pillow. She did not. Once better, I was immediately doing my usual jobs around St Michael's, polishing floors, looking after Eugene, and doing messages for the nuns. One evening as I was polishing the boots, not long after being sick, I developed a severe earache, but was afraid to say anything in case I would be accused of trying to get back into sick bay or escape doing my jobs. It was difficult to concentrate as the pain intensified. I cried as I polished the boots, occasionally rubbing my ear violently.

'What is the crying for, Pat Doyle?' Mother Paul asked.

'I have a pain in my ear, Mother.'

'You are just over the measles – you couldn't have a pain.'

'But I have, Mother, honest,' I pleaded.

She admonished me, suggesting that if I concentrated more on what I was doing the pain would vanish.

'Offer it up for the Holy Souls in Purgatory,' she said before leaving me to finish the boots.

In bed the pain worsened. I pulled at my ear and swayed my head from side to side in an attempt to get relief. Eventually I screamed: 'My ear, it's killing me.'

Mother Paul ran into the dormitory.

'Jesus, Mary and Joseph, child,' she exclaimed, 'what in God's name are you trying to do?'

'I can't help it,' I said.

'You'll get nothing for the pain until you stop that crying,' she insisted.

'I can't.'

'You better try a little harder.'

I managed to control my crying long enough for her to get some tablets, which she gave me from her hand.

'Drink this,' she said, handing me a tin mug containing a mixture of warm milk and porter which I found difficult to take. The taste sickened me and I was certain I would vomit.

'I think I'm going to be sick,' I said.

'If you vomit, my lad, you will lie in it for the night.'

Not long after taking the tablets and the drink, I went into a deep sleep.

When I woke the next morning it was to feel Mother Paul's hand resting on my forehead. She asked about the pain and whether it was gone.

'Yes, Mother,' I answered.

She took my head in her hands and tilted it to one side to look into my ears.

'Is it any wonder,' she exclaimed, 'that you have earache. Those ears are filthy, absolutely filthy!'

She took some cotton wool and a tweezers from a small box, wrapped the tip in cotton wool and probed into my ear, removing the accumulated wax. Then she gave me two more tablets. They began to dissolve on my tongue. I stuck it out to show her the difficulty I was having trying to swallow them. She rushed into her room and returned with a glass of water. I drank quickly until the taste of the tablets was gone, then I went more slowly, enjoying the cold smoothness of the glass.

'Come on,' the impatient nun said, 'hurry up.'

I gulped down the remaining mouthful of water. It was the first time in my life I had been given a glass to drink from.

A month or two later I was given the duties of senior altar boy for a High Mass. Throughout the week I was excited and careful not to bring any trouble upon myself which would jeopardize the chance I had so often thought about. At play time I got together with some other boys to practise serving. Walking with solemn slowness and carrying imaginary missals I rehearsed every move. I genuflected reverently, barely touching the concrete yard with my right knee as I gave the proper responses to the prayers being mumbled by another boy who was acting as priest.

In preparation for Benediction I pretended to swing the thurible. My hands swayed gently, ensuring that the imaginary instrument gave off just the right amount of incense. I rang imaginary bells, not too loud: that might annoy the Bishop. I visualized him holding the gold monstrance aloft, the white host in its centre, and I swung my thurible, head bowed in the presence of God. I had always been told never to look at the host for longer than a couple of seconds as it would be irreverent to do otherwise. I sang the Tantum Ergo, softly to myself. Sunday would be for real. No pretending. Though I was nervous I was also excited.

On Sunday morning I got up early and dressed in the clothes which had been left out for me by the nuns, before washing my face and hands in cold water. I dried them with a coarse piece of white cloth which hurt my face when I rubbed it. So that I could receive communion, I had nothing to eat or drink.

I walked quickly through the town, weaving in and out between couples on their way to Mass. The men were dressed in their Sunday suits and their shoes shone in the early morning sunlight. The women too were dressed in their best clothes. Bright coloured dresses covered by darker coloured overcoats, with stiletto heels tapping sharply on the pavement. Most of them wore scarves, some had white or black mantillas held on by a single strand – the clip hidden in their permed hair.

The altar was brightly lit and almost overcrowded with brass and cut-glass vases containing a variety of flowers. Colourful carnations and leafy ferns lined each side of the steps leading up to it. The red carpet, cross-shaped, and held in position by brass bars looked even redder than usual. The dome-shaped brass gong stood out majestically on its white marble pedestal. The sacristan, usually clad in just a black soutane, wore a bright red one and a pure white surplice.

There were sixteen altar boys, all dressed in red and white. Just before Mass began the sacristan asked me to bring the red missal and brass stand to the altar. Positioning it carefully to the right of the tabernacle, I tidied the coloured marking-ribbons so they hung neatly down onto the white altar cloth. I returned to the sacristy and took my place at the head of one of the rows of eight boys.

The congregation stood as we walked slowly onto the altar followed by the priests and finally the Bishop. Each of the servers took his position at the bottom step as the Bishop went to the centre of the altar to begin the sacred ritual. Two priests helped as the Bishop put three measures of incense into the thurible which I held open. Once he was finished I allowed the silver lid to slip slowly into the closed position before handing it to a priest, who passed it to the Bishop. With great solemnity, the celebrant swung it gently towards each part of the altar. A blessing, or perhaps an exorcism. The con-celebrants blessed each other before returning the thurible to me. The Bishop stood before me on the highest step of the altar, as I knelt on the lowest and gently swung the thurible at him.

The organist struck a single chord and, after a momentary silence, the Bishop chanted the opening lines of a prayer before the voices of the choir filled the church with the appropriate response. He sat while one of the priests read the epistle. I watched closely waiting for the moment he would lay his hand on the altar cloth, an indication that he was nearing the end of the reading and a signal to me to ascend the steps from the side and move the missal to the Gospel side of the altar.

I lifted the missal and stand, bowed and prepared to descend the centre steps. On the second step I tripped and fell face down. I watched helplessly as the missal slid across the polished mosaic floor, its ribbons trailing like the tail of some exotic bird. The noise of the stand reverberated through the silent church. I could feel every pair of eyes on me as I got to my feet to collect the missal. Several of the priests who were con-celebrating pushed me away, discreetly whispering to me to go back and kneel in my place. There were many minutes of silence as the ribbons were replaced at the appropriate pages. I watched, disgusted that something like this should have happened. I knew the nuns from the school would be at Mass and was certain I would be in the worst possible trouble. I prayed. Eventually I was overcome by fear and fainted.

When I came to, Mother Paul and Mother Michael were standing over me. Just as one was about to say something to me, a priest came into the sacristy. I was petrified. He stretched out his hand, placed it gently on my shoulder and asked if I was all right.

'Yes, Father,' I answered.

'What happened was an accident,' he said, 'there's nothing to worry about.'

As soon as he was gone, Mother Michael said, 'You have disgraced Saint Michael's.'

'I didn't mean it,' I replied.

'Let me tell you this,' Mother Paul said sternly, 'and remember it. You will never ever again set foot inside an altar rails.'

She could not have known it at the time but her words were prophetic.

As the rest of the boys took off their vestments in the sacristy, Mother Paul left saying she would deal with me later. Some of the boys played handball after Mass and I decided to join in, but was told to 'get lost'. They jeered me for falling and then fainting. When they saw that I was almost crying they became even more vocal in their taunting. 'Orphan, orphan,' they jeered as I walked from the churchyard. As they continued to jeer I became enraged and ran back towards them, kicking and punching as many as I could. The sacristan rushed from the sacristy and pulled me off one boy I was threatening to kill. I was shaking with anger, shocked by my sudden outburst of temper. I wondered briefly if the sacristan would tell the nuns about the incident, before deciding I didn't care.

I walked through the town, hands in my pockets and head bowed, desperately aware of being watched by the entire community. Down the street Mother Paul was waiting.

'Get your hands out of your pockets and lift up your head, God knows you're bad enough. You're a disgrace to yourself, worse still, you're a disgrace to the school.'

Hard as she tried, she could not keep her voice down and it rose gradually with every word. People passing looked at her, then at me.

'If you had lifted your feet the way I have been telling you to, none of this would have happened, but you didn't. No, you made a fool of yourself and you brought disgrace on all of us.' She reminded me for the second time that I would never set foot inside the rails of an altar again but this time she added, 'as long as I am alive.' She jabbed me with her sharp pointed finger and made me walk in front of her.

'Lift your head, put back your shoulders and in the name of Almighty God will you lift that foot of yours,' she said.

On Sunday afternoon visitors came to St Michael's. They were usually relations of some of the nuns or well-to-do people from the locality. Very occasionally a relation of one of the boys would turn up. When visitors did arrive we were expected to provide entertainment for them by singing or putting on a short play. I felt important being on show. I always sang the same songs: 'A Mother's Love is a Blessing' or 'Two Little Orphans', which delighted the nuns and their guests. Mother Michael smiled while playing the piano and scowled if I didn't reach the notes as she liked me to.

Everyone clapped politely when I was finished and I bowed to them as I had been trained to do. If there was time we would put on a short play, *Tweedledum and*

Tweedledee that finished with all of us singing 'Little Mister Baggy Britches'. Some people laughed out loud while others smiled politely. When the show was finished, a trolley containing china cups, and plates stacked with cakes was brought into the hall. We remained on the stage as the visitors ate and drank. The voice of John McCormack singing 'Ave Maria' crackled through the horn of the black gramophone at the side of the stage, which Miss Sharpe wound up before lowering the heavy needle onto the record's edge. She quietly warned us not to stare at people eating, then, as she stood out of sight of nuns and visitors, she spoke about McCormack's sweet voice and the crispness of his diction. A clear voice that never missed a note or lacked breath. He opened his mouth when he sung, he took deep breaths, he didn't sing through his teeth or his nose. His voice flowed, never wavering.

It was not uncommon for Miss Sharpe to become completely carried away as she listened to her favourite singer. Whenever she was minding us she used to put his records on and it was at such times that some of us would take the opportunity to try and look up her skirt. Quiet arguments arose about the colour of her knickers. We'd dare each other to look up her skirt, taking turns, nervous of being caught.

I had been given a miraculous medal for my Communion. As Mother Paul put the silver medal with its blue string, around my neck, she reminded me of its significance. It was the symbol of purity and chastity. I used to take it off, and slide it across the floor as near to Miss Sharpe's feet as I could get it. As she stood entranced by the music I'd pick up the medal and at the same time look up her skirt. If she did notice me I was certain I would be able to explain my presence by saying that I had dropped the medal. Afterwards we'd group together and laugh at what we had seen.

There were times when she wouldn't notice the record had finished or that we were all talking. She'd become annoyed when she realized we were not in the least interested in the music and order us out into the yard, apparently unperturbed by the fact that it was raining heavily.

'It's spilling,' I'd say, pointing to the windows.

'Get out,' she'd shout, 'a drop of rain is not going to kill you.'

I ran around the wet yard, chasing leaves that had been prematurely blown down or skidding into wet and slimy clusters of them, enjoying trying to remain upright and laughing when I landed arse first on the ground.

There was one part of the yard that was always dry because a section of the building protruded out over it. Here I would squat down on my haunches and with my arms outstretched get two other boys to pull me along the concrete. In the twilight, or winter dark, the studs on the soles and heels of my boots would leave a trail of sparks in their wake. Causing sparks was one of the things I enjoyed doing most. To create them I had to run as fast as I could and kick the heel of one boot hard against the ground.

Like many of the other boys I often came in from the yard with my hair plastered flat down onto my head and my clothes soaked, but nobody seemed to care. It was not uncommon for us to sit and eat our evening meal with rain water dripping from our clothing onto the dining hall floor.

CHAPTER FIVE

In May 1958 most of the older boys in the school were told to write to a relative. Many of us had never met the people we were being asked to write to, and even if we did, couldn't remember them. The letter writing was supervised by Mother Michael, the nun responsible for our schooling, and their purpose was to ask for a two week holiday away from St Michael's. All the letters were written under her close supervision.

She told me to write to my aunt Mary. I looked at her, surprised.

'Don't look so stunned,' she said, 'you do have an aunt as well as an uncle.'

It was three years since I had arrived in the school and though I remembered my uncle, I had never heard of any aunt. Mother Michael wrote a standard letter on the blackboard which she instructed us to copy. The address was in the top right hand corner and the date underneath.

'Dear . . .' she had written, telling us that 'the blank line is for you to fill the name of the person to whom you are writing.'

'*Dear Aunt Mary*,' I wrote, before looking at the blackboard to copy what was written on it.

'*I hope you are well as I am myself, thank Dog. I would like to come and spend a fortnight with you if you would not mind. I will be good, and do everything I am told. Mother Michael and Mother Paul send you their good wishes. I am very happy here, the nuns are very good to me. I pray for you every night. I look forward to hearing from you soon,*

   I remain,

   Your nephew,

   Patrick.'

Mother Michael went around checking the letters. She slapped her wooden ruler down on the desk of one of the boys near me. It made a sharp crack which startled the other boys.

'Always a capital G for God,' she shouted.

She picked up my letter, and asked me to spell God.

'G.O.D.' I answered confidently. She walked to the top of the classroom with my letter in her hand.

'This is more of this fellow's clowning,' she said. 'Not only does he tell lies and bring the school into disrepute, now he has taken to making fun of God Himself.' I watched her face redden as she rushed towards my desk. Thinking she was going to hit me, I cowered. She banged her clenched fist on the desk.

'Spell God,' she demanded again.

'G.O.D.' I said.

She handed me the letter and asked me to read the first sentence. As soon as I looked at it I realized my mistake. I reached for my pen to correct it.

'Read,' she shouted.

'Dear Aunt Mary,

I hope you are well as I am myself, thank Dog.' Some of the boys laughed, but stopped suddenly when she said there was nothing to laugh about. She referred to what I had

75

written as blasphemy, one of the most serious of all sins. Kneeling at the top of the classroom, I was forced to say an 'Act of Contrition' before being given six slaps, three on each hand. Then I collected all the letters and left them on her table.

I was startled the day Mother Paul told me my uncle was coming to bring me for a two week holiday to my aunt's house in Wexford. I was uncertain about whether I wanted to go or not. On the one hand I was delighted to get away from the almost constant punishment, but on the other I knew I would miss the companionship of the boys. Because I knew nothing about my aunt I was nervous of having to spend a holiday with her. Life in Saint Michael's was by now familiar. I had come to accept it as normal.

It was a Sunday. Breakfast was served at eight o'clock instead of seven which allowed time to get to early Mass beforehand. I waited in line with the rest of the boys to have my dish filled with porridge from a heavy stainless steel cauldron. I walked carefully to my place, carrying my bowl with my eyes fixed on its floating contents. My steps were slow and deliberate, I didn't want to spill it. Having eaten the porridge and scraped the bowl clean, I passed the dish to the boy beside who passed his on until there was a pile of dishes stacked at the end of the long table. The nun in charge of the kitchen served cocoa and bread, and when breakfast was finished, four boys were sent to the scullery to wash up. Any other day I would almost certainly have been one of the four, but as I was going on holidays I had to keep myself clean which meant that I didn't have to do any work at all.

At dinner time I was not allowed to eat with my companions. I was told to remain in the yard where I walked around wondering what my holiday was going to be like. I looked up towards the top floor of the L-shaped building to the statue of the Sacred Heart. Even in the bright sunlight the building looked cold and grey. I quietly walked up the fire escape so that I could see into the dining hall. Everyone was eating. The orchard was at the other end of the yard. I had often noticed the nuns walking through it as they said their prayers. I walked to its railings and pressed my face tightly against the black bars, almost putting my head through. Amongst the trees and bushes I saw the familiar limping figure of Mr O'Rourke. He was dressed in a dark blue suit with a heavy grey stripe through it. He saw me and immediately came forward.

'Well, be the hokey, aren't you the real smasher today?' I told him I was going away to stay with my aunt for two weeks. He bent his wrinkled face low towards me and said, 'Sure won't it be grand for ye to have a bit of a holiday. I wouldn't mind an ould holiday away from them nuns meself.' He laughed. 'Now,' he continued, 'for a fella that's going on his holidays, ye don't look all that happy.'

Before I could answer he slipped his wrinkled hand through the railings and unfolded it.

'Go on,' he urged, 'them's a grand goosegog, not sour like they were the last time. Why aren't ye having the dinner?'

'I'm going to have it with the nuns when my uncle comes.'

The old man's face beamed, his smile revealing the only two teeth he had, both badly decayed.

'Dinner with the nuns, begob. Them's the people that knows how to feed ye, china cups and plates and the best of silver. I had me own dinner with them a couple of times and I can tell ye this, 'tis better than I'd ever get at home. Make the best of it, it's not often you'll get the chance.' I nodded. He turned his back to me and looked round the orchard. 'When I started here there was nothing, only them goosegog bushes.' I could feel his pride as he looked around at the apple and pear trees. 'Them gravel paths weren't there either, now begob the nuns is using them for praying on. I wonder do they ever think of me while they're sayin' the rosary.' Before we parted, he told me that while I was away my feet would grow, and I would have to have the boots fixed again when I got back. Then he limped away through the fruit trees and out of sight. By early afternoon I was hungry and growing more anxious at the thought of going to stay with someone I didn't know. I tried to get into the pantry for a slice of bread but my nerve failed. I was afraid of being caught and each time decided it wouldn't be worth the risk. I waited in the yard for my uncle. By three o'clock I felt weak and had cramps in my stomach, by four the pain was unbearable and I cried. Mother Paul noticed me.

'What's the crying about now?'

'I'm hungry, Mother, and I have pains in my stomach.'

'Don't be ridiculous,' she said. 'Offer it up for the black babies out in Africa who never get a bit to eat. Go to the kitchen and wait until your uncle comes. The last thing the poor man wants is to turn up and find you crying like a baby.'

The kitchen was hot and filled with steam. The sun shone through a window that looked out onto a yard packed with cardboard boxes laden with the withered leaves of cabbage and galvanized bins overflowing with other food debris. The cook, a small rotund figure, took little notice of me beyond casting the occasional glance over the top of her glasses. I tried to ensure I was not in her way. She wore a white apron over her black habit and had her sleeves rolled up. I watched as she mixed a large bowl of flour and water, her red face perspiring continuously as she used her apron to wipe it. She scattered flour over a rectangular board and tossed a big lump of dough onto it, kneading it vigorously until it was ready for baking.

The kitchen door opened and Mother Paul signalled to me. I went towards her and we walked to a room in the convent where my uncle was waiting.

'And you thought he was never going to come?' she said, smiling at my uncle. Three years had passed since I had last seen him.

'Are you not going to greet your uncle?' she asked.

'Hello,' I said.

He stretched out his hand and took mine. His grip was loose and nervous. His face was tanned, weathered, and deeply wrinkled while his hands looked rough though his skin was soft. Every few seconds, he rubbed his almost bald head with his right hand, and as he did, I noticed it was pitted with tiny black marks.

'We'll go and have something to eat, Mr Furlong,' Mother Paul said. 'You must be hungry. I know one little man who certainly is.' She walked between us along polished corridors to the dining room, opened its oak door and invited my uncle to go in. He stood aside and insisted that she go in first. She gave both of us a chair at the circular table covered in a white cloth. I noticed the delicate china cups and saucers that Mr O'Rourke had referred to. There were silver knives and forks and spoons. A small round straw basket in the centre of the table contained fruit which was stacked in a pyramid and decorated at the edges with green and black grapes.

'I'm just going to leave you for a second,' Mother Paul said. 'I want to get some of the other nuns to join us.' During the short time I was alone with my uncle neither of us spoke. Mother Paul returned with two other nuns which she introduced to him but not to me. They sat down and made polite conversation with my uncle who seemed distinctly ill at ease, never sure of what to say. Before eating the nuns said grace. I joined in but my uncle just kept his head bowed. We had soup first, the adults taking theirs from a bowl while I was given a half-filled cup. For dinner there was bacon and cabbage with potatoes.

'Eat up, Pat,' Mother Paul kept saying to me, and though I was hungry it was hard to eat. The system I had become used to was gone and I was tense and nervous without it. When the nuns spoke about the weather my uncle answered them, otherwise he said very little but listened intently as Mother Paul spoke of how I was getting on in school.

'He is a very bright child and I can say that he is a credit to us.' She did not say anything else about me and I was relieved. After dinner she asked my uncle if he would like to wash his hands while she took me to the toilet. The toilet was spotless and the air laden with the scent of disinfectant. The walls were tiled up to the ceiling and there was white tissue hanging from a chrome toilet roll holder. I undid my trousers and sat up on the toilet bowl. Mother Paul stood in front of me urging me to make sure I 'went'.

'You have a long journey ahead and you can't expect to be stopping every few miles just because you want to go to the toilet.' I sat there, my hands firmly gripping the seat. I clenched my fists and gritted my teeth as I willed my bowels to empty. After much forcing I succeeded and then stood up to refasten my trousers.

'Wipe yourself,' Mother Paul snapped before she realized that I had no idea of what she meant. She took a small piece of tissue from the roll and folded it in two. 'Every time you go to the toilet, you must wipe your backside. Don't forget that.' In my time in St Michael's I never used toilet paper but just pulled my trousers up when finished.

We returned to the dining room and Mother Paul's face beamed.

'I think he's ready for the journey now, Mr Furlong,' she said, looking at the clock on the mantelpiece. 'I'm sure you'll want to be getting away.' My uncle thanked her and the other nuns for the dinner, before she accompanied us to a black Morris Minor waiting outside the convent. There was a man sitting in the driver's seat.

'You should have come in and had something to eat,' Mother Paul said.

'Not at all, Mother,' he said. I had never heard an adult use the word 'mother' to address a nun before.

'Are you sure you won't come in and have just a cup of tea?'

'No, Mother, no. Thanks very much all the same, but I won't.' I got into the back of the car and my uncle sat in the front passenger seat. The engine started and slowly the car moved away. Mother Paul waved and as I looked back at her, I saw her lips mime 'be good'.

We gradually gathered speed along the road I had so often walked. I sat silently, looking through the windows at people out for their Sunday walks. The sun was getting lower in the sky. Both the driver and my uncle pulled their peaked caps down so as to shade their eyes. The towns and villages we drove through were strangely quiet. Mothers watched from their front doors, shouting occasionally at any of the children who were in danger of getting their Sunday clothes soiled.

'How are ye doing?' my uncle asked.

'Fine,' I answered. 'What time will we get there?'

'It's about three hours journey,' he said, and the driver nodded to confirm that. My uncle spoke to him.

'We might get to stop somewhere along the way.'

'Aye,' the driver said. Then they both got into conversation about farming and horses, cows and milking, and then hurling and football.

During that journey my uncle must have remembered the last time we had travelled along the same road. He could never have forgotten my pitiful cries and my attempts to break free of the person holding on to me in the back seat. He must have remembered my kicking at the interior panels of the car, hysterical at being taken away from where I had spent the early part of my life. Looking back now, my presence must have brought back many frightening and nightmarish things to him. How he had discovered my father hanging and his own incapacity to console me as I roamed around the farm screaming, with my face marked from rubbing and my clothes dirty and wet. The young girl who happened to be passing the gate of the farmyard whom he had pleaded with to go and get help without telling what he needed it for. The guards, the doctor and the priest. The coroner's court where he had to relive the sordid business over again before the coroner pronounced that Patrick Doyle had died from asphyxiation due to hanging.

The car stopped and my uncle suggested we get out for something to drink and 'maybe a bit to eat'. We went into a public house, filled with men having their Sunday evening drink. A dense pall of cigarette smoke hung in the air. The chattering of the various groups fused into one cacophonous sound. Both men ordered their drinks at the bar while I took a seat at a small wooden table. My uncle brought me down a large bottle of lemonade and a bag of potato crisps before joining his friend at the bar.

After a few drinks the two men went to the toilet and I followed them. The stench of stale urine was choking, ammonia catching my breath. I was unsure of how to use the toilets so I waited for my uncle to start. As he undid his buttons, so did I. I copied his movements as he shuffled nearer the urinal and thought it unusual that he made no effort to prevent me from seeing his penis. I watched him hold it and withdraw the foreskin. At first I had difficulty in passing any water at all and it was only when I heard the sound next to me that I relaxed enough to be able to go to the toilet. When he was finished he shook his penis vigorously before replacing it in his trousers and buttoning his flies.

I watched as the two men poured black porter from brown bottles into sparkling clean glasses. A dirty-looking yellowish froth formed on top and when this reached the top of the glass they stopped pouring. They sat looking at their drinks like two priests about to offer wine up to God during Mass. My uncle nodded to me. I drank the lemonade slowly, its tingling sensation a new experience for me. He walked down from the counter and handed me a large bar of chocolate. I took it and thanked him. The two men lifted their glasses slowly, their mouths hugging the rims as they poured the porter down. They had four drinks and I finished the large bottle of Taylor Keith before we all went to the toilet and resumed our journey. By the time we reached Wexford town it was getting dark. Lights shone from houses where people had not yet drawn the curtains. The narrowness of the streets amazed me and I told my uncle so. 'What time is it when two cars meet on the main street in Wexford?' he asked, as the driver and himself laughed.

'I don't know,' I answered.

'Tin to tin.'

The car turned into a sleepy cul-de-sac and came to a halt outside a whitewashed, pebble-dashed, semi-detached house. There were brass fittings on the red hall door with the number six above the letter box. White lace curtains hung partially open on the windows. My uncle got out of the car, opened the little iron gate and walked up the narrow concrete path to the front door. I watched as he waited for an answer to his knock. An old woman opened the door and shook his hand. They chatted for a while before he came back to the car and let me out. I didn't like the look of the woman, there was something about the entire situation that made me desperately want to be back in St Michael's.

In the neat parlour, she offered my uncle a cup of tea which she poured from a decorative silver teapot. She gave me a glass of milk and a plain biscuit. They chatted to one another while I looked around the room at the various statues that sat in every available space. My aunt looked at me and remarked to my uncle that I didn't have much to say. 'He's a quiet lad anyway and it'll take him a few days to settle in,' he replied.

My aunt had long grey hair which she kept tied up in a neat bun at the back of her head. I watched her fingers tremble as she lifted the cup to her thin lips. The purple veins in her hands showed through her wrinkled flesh. They were prominent and lumpy looking. Her knuckles where white and swollen. She had difficulty in pouring tea and in lifting her own cup to drink. On the finger of her left hand a shining gold wedding ring had embedded itself into her aging skin. Instead of shoes, she had pink slippers on her feet. She moved slowly as she gathered the cups and saucers to bring them to the kitchen. My uncle rose from his chair and told her that he would call some day and take me to the shops. Then he wished me good luck and left. She walked to the hall door with him and waved as he drove away from the front of the house.

'Now,' she said as she came back into the room, 'I think it is time for bed, but before that we will say our night prayers. I'm sure you say yours every night in the School.'

'I do,' I answered. She opened the drawer of one of the cabinets and took out a black Rosary beads. She held the crucifix in her hand, looked at it and blessed herself, pressing it to her forehead, her breast and each of her

84

shoulders. She moved a chair from under the table and used it for support as she knelt on the carpeted floor. Once I was kneeling she began the Rosary.

'In the name of the Father, and of the Son, and of the Holy Ghost. Thou, O Lord, will open my lips.' She looked crossly at me when I didn't answer.

'Do you know the Rosary at all?' she snapped.

'I know the Our Father, the Hail Mary and the Glory be to the Father,' I replied.

'And my tongue shall announce His praise,' she answered herself before starting into the Five Joyful Mysteries – the Resurrection, the Ascension and so on. Ten Hail Marys for each, sandwiched between an Our Father and a Glory be to the Father. She said the first half of each prayer and I the second. At first I was nervous and my voice trembled but I became more confident as I went along.

After the Rosary she led me up the softly-carpeted stairs to the bedroom. It was spotlessly clean and sparsely furnished with just a single bed and a two-drawer wooden dresser. There was a silver-framed picture of the Blessed Virgin on the wall.

'You better go to the bathroom,' she said, pushing open one of the doors that led off the small landing.

'Wash yourself and be sure to go to the toilet.' When I came out she was waiting in my room. There was a man's shirt on my bed which she told me to wear to bed. I began to undress by taking off my jumper and shirt. I was just going to drop my trousers when she said: 'Wait! Put on this first.' She held the shirt over my head and told me I must be modest always. I got into bed, immediately noticing the softness of the mattress and the freshness of the sheets and pillow cover. My aunt left the door open, and the landing light on. In the next room I heard her moving about, opening and shutting presses and drawers. When I heard her door open I closed my eyes and pretended to be asleep. She stood looking into my room before turning to go to the bathroom, leaving the door open after her. I could see her long grey hair brushed straight down almost to her waist. Her back was stooped and her pale skin contrasted sharply with the dark colour of her dressing gown. When she emerged from the bathroom she was carrying a glass of water with her false teeth in it. Her appearance frightened me, particularly her sunken cheeks, and I prayed that I could go back to the other boys. I slept fitfully that night, aware that the person I was staying with fitted my idea of a banshee. As I tried to sleep I had the very real feeling that I had been in the house before and that this woman had been a part of my earlier life.

Outside the rain beat against the window. I looked towards the curtains and watched them swell slightly in the breeze that pierced the gaps in the window. My aunt coughed, a feeble rattling cough. I turned around in my bed, then turned the pillow. Its coolness relaxed me and I drifted into sleep.

The morning sun shone into the room through a gap in the curtains. Birds whistled and chirped. I wanted to get up but I felt it would be the wrong thing to do. I was used to being told when to get up so I decided to stay in bed until I was called. Eventually she called my name from the bottom of the stairs. As I dressed, strange smells and sounds attracted my attention. Sizzling and a kind of spitting. It was only when I got down to the kitchen that I discovered what the smells were. My aunt's hair was neatly pinned in a bun again as she cooked breakfast. I stood beside her for a moment and watched.

'What are they?' I asked. She looked at me.

'Do you not know?' she asked.

'No.'

'Rasher, sausage and egg,' she said. 'Now go over to the table and get yourself some cornflakes.' From a box on the table I spilled some into a bowl and began to eat them.

'Why didn't you put some milk and sugar on them?' she asked as she poured some from a white jug with a blue line around the neck of it.

'I never had these before,' I said. She took little notice of what I said. I had difficulty trying to eat the fry as I had never used a knife or fork before. Everything I had eaten up to now was taken off a spoon. My aunt offered me tea which I took out of curiosity, before deciding I didn't like it. She gave me a glass of milk instead. As we walked to church she told me that every morning for twenty years, since her husband died, she had gone to Mass, no matter how bad the weather was. She didn't always go to communion because she found the long fast beforehand 'a bit much'. She was dressed in a heavy black coat and hat with a huge pin through it. She explained to people she met that I was an orphan staying with her for a fortnight's holidays. They patted my head and remarked that I was a great boy all the same.

After Mass she did her shopping, calling to the butcher's first and asking him for a 'nice piece of bacon'. He wrapped it in brown paper, tied it with string, then handed it to me. I was glad to get out of the shop. I felt sick at the sight of carcasses of cows and pigs hanging from hooks on tubular steel bars, and the bloodstained aprons of the men serving behind the counter. Next we went to the greengrocers where she spent a long time talking to another woman about me. Every few seconds the women looked down and when my aunt realized I was listening, she reprimanded me. The woman asked her what my parents died from and she replied that my mother had died of a heart attack and my father the same way shortly afterwards.

This was the first time I heard how my parents died, and though it seemed to have great significance for the woman it made no impact on me.

In the newsagents my aunt was greeted by name. Without having to ask for anything, the girl behind the counter handed her a copy of the *Wexford People* with her name written in biro in the top right hand corner. A woman who noticed me looking through the comics asked me to pick one.

My aunt interrupted saying, 'Pat doesn't mind what he gets.'

The lady pressed me again to choose a comic.

'*The Eagle*,' I said.

'Did he say thanks?' my aunt asked.

'Of course he did.'

There was a steep hill from the town up to my aunt's house, and she had great difficulty in walking up. Every few minutes she stopped to catch her breath. I became worried at one point because she seemed to be a long time holding on to a railing and my anxiety must have registered with her because she said, 'Don't worry, it's just that I'm not as young as I used to be.' I was carrying all the messages but I didn't mind. I would have done anything to ensure that nothing happened to her while I was there. When we got back to the cul-de-sac where she lived she told me to go and play with the rest of the children who lived on the street. I was reluctant and, pretending I didn't hear her, opened the gate leading to the house and walked quickly up the narrow concrete path. I waited for her to open the hall door.

'You go out and play,' she said again. 'I'm going in to have a rest and I'll call you when dinner is ready.'

I watched the other children. A boy on a tricycle was racing a girl on a scooter. There was a lot of noise as the boys cheered for the boy and the girls for the girl. When the race was over and they had crossed the imaginary line they began to jeer at each other, disputing who had won.

A dark-haired, fresh-faced girl approached me. 'Did you see the race?'

'Yes,' I said.

'Who won?' she asked.

I pointed to the girl on the scooter and the girls cheered. The boys, annoyed at my judgement, began to jeer.

'Look at the stupid clothes he has on him,' they laughed.

The girl who had spoken to me in the first instance told them to 'shut up'.

'Look at his big farmer's boots,' they jeered again.

'Shut up,' the girl pleaded again.

'He's just a sissy,' they taunted.

I was so different from them. I was dressed in a grey heavy suit which I was given in the Industrial School. It was dreary and drab-looking compared to their bright cotton colours. Many of them were in their bare feet or in leather sandals. Eventually they agreed to let me play with them. The boy who owned the tricycle asked me if I would like a go on it but I declined. I didn't want to make a total fool of myself by demonstrating my inability to ride it. Then they wanted me to race with them but I refused even though I was a good runner and had won races in school. I often ran in heavy boots before but was not prepared to do so now in case they jeered again.

'What's your name?' the dark-haired girl asked.

'Pat,' I said.

'Does everyone call you Pat?'

'Mostly.'

'My daddy's name is Patrick but everyone calls him Pat except my mammy. What's your daddy's name?'

'He's dead,' I answered, and before she could ask any more questions told her that my mother was dead too and I

89

was just on holidays with my aunt Mary for a fortnight.

'What's your name?' I asked.

'Well,' she said, 'my real name is Maria but everyone calls me Ria.'

'Where do you live?' she asked.

'In an orphanage. It's a good bit away from here, my uncle said it was about ninety miles.'

'Who minds you?'

'Nuns do.'

'I hate nuns, they're always giving out,' she said.

'Sometimes they're cross and sometimes they're all right.'

My aunt called me for dinner and I left Ria, promising to be out again later. As soon as I got into the house I asked my aunt if I could go back out when I had my dinner eaten.

'No,' she said, 'I want to bring you up to the convent to see your sister Ann.'

It was the first time in my life that anybody had ever told me I had a sister.

CHAPTER SIX

My sister was just over two years old when my mother died, aged forty-two, from cancer of the breast. She was taken into an orphanage in Wexford, run by the Sisters of Mercy, where she remained until her mid-teens. She would have been five the first evening I saw her.

Having washed up after dinner my aunt brought me to the bathroom where she cleaned my face and combed my hair. She told me to sit in a chair in the parlour and wait until she was ready. I watched her check in the mirror over the mantelpiece to see if her face was all right and her hat was on properly. As she was tidying loose strands of her hair she muttered about my uncle never being around when he was needed.

'How far is it to the convent?' I asked.

She sighed wearily. 'A mile, or maybe a bit more.' It was a hot sunny day and I knew that she did not like having to walk so far. I hoped she would decide not to go.

We walked along a country road, bounded by hedgerows and broken occasionally by a half-built house or an old-fashioned bungalow. My aunt hardly spoke at all. She allowed me to walk ahead of her and as I did I wondered again what my sister was like. Would she know me or I know her? What would I say to her? I didn't even know then if she was younger or older than me.

The green bushes of the country road merged into a high granite wall. My aunt called me and brushed my suit down with the palms of her gloved hands. She took off one glove and spat gently onto her hand before pressing my hair down. She warned me to be on my best behaviour. I could hear the sounds of children playing, their screams breaking the silence of the countryside. My aunt held my hand firmly and walked through the wrought iron gates of Saint Mary's Orphanage for Girls.

As we crossed the yard everything became quiet. The girls stared at us.

'Who are you looking for, Miss?' one of them asked.

'The nun,' my aunt answered.

The girl ran off and I felt embarrassed standing in the yard with so many girls watching me. I wondered if one of them was my sister. A nun in the familiar habit of the Sisters of Mercy rushed out of a single-storey building to one side of the yard and came towards us. As she walked I could hear her telling the girls to get on with whatever they were doing. She shook my aunt's hand warmly and after some minutes of conversation between them, the nun told one of the girls to get Ann Doyle.

'Come to see your sister, have you?'

'Yes, Mother,' I said.

As we walked towards the convent door two girls approached us. The nun indicated to one of them to go away. Then she smiled at me. 'Well, this is your sister, have you nothing to say to her?'

We stared at each other.

'Are the pair of ye just going to stand there gaping at each other or have ye lost ye're tongues?' the nun said.

She suggested to my aunt that we be left together and

both of them went into the convent.

In the school yard we tried to say something to one another but it was difficult. We did not know each other and were conscious of the girls watching us. My sister was very pretty. She had fair hair which had been put in ringlets. She wore a lovely daintily patterned dress and a white cardigan that was a few sizes too big for her. We didn't speak but when someone suggested a game of chasing we both joined in. The girls yelled as I pursued them. I ran after my sister and, when I caught her, shouted: 'You're out.' She looked disappointed and was on the verge of tears. A bigger girl suggested that she should have a second chance because she was my sister, and was smaller than me. I was pleased.

The nun and my aunt came out of the convent and the game stopped immediately. She called my sister and I to her and asked if we had found anything to talk about.

'Not really, Mother,' I said.

'You don't mean to tell me that you have nothing to say to your sister after all the years ye have been away from each other.'

My aunt tried to encourage me to say something but the words would not come. The years had created a great distance between us and we were being asked to bridge it in a short time. My sister's pale, freckled face reddened shyly as she smiled revealing two prominent front teeth.

'As sure as God,' the nun said, 'there's no doubt but they are brother and sister.'

'Oh without a doubt,' my aunt agreed.

A sudden shower sent the girls scurrying for cover into the sheds on either side of the yard and instinctively I followed them. The nun and my aunt dashed back into the convent. In the rush to get out of the rain I sat on a bench beside my sister and, without realizing it, we began talking to each other.

'Do you like it here?' I asked.

'Yes,' she replied, 'sometimes.'

She and some of the other girls remarked on how I addressed the nun as 'Mother'. They laughed and said they always referred to the nuns as 'Sister'.

'Do you ever get hit or sent to bed without any supper?' I asked.

'Only if you're really bold.'

'I'm always getting hit and locked in the coal shed. Once I got locked into the boiler house.'

'The big girls get slapped sometimes,' she said, 'but not the little ones.'

'It doesn't matter if you are big or small in our school, you still get slapped,' I replied, before a group of bigger girls joined in our conversation.

'I got slapped once for not having the laces of my shoes tied right. I wouldn't like to tell you where they slapped me,' one girl said, laughing.

She didn't have to. I knew.

When the rain stopped we played chasing again and in the middle of the game the nun and my aunt Mary emerged into the bright sunlight. I walked towards them and the nun insisted that my sister come with me.

'Have the pair of ye made friends?' she asked.

'Yes, Mother,' I answered.

'And will you come and see Ann again before you finish your holidays?'

My aunt said that I would. As I was about to leave St Mary's the nun suggested that I kiss my sister goodbye. I was embarrassed and very conscious of the older girls giggling. I refused to do so.

'Sure he has a girlfriend across the road from me,' my aunt said.

'Is that what he's up to? Wait till I tell Mother Paul.' Both of them laughed but I was terrified that something would be said about my friendship with Ria.

'Now he's no good, Mrs Boyle, is he? He wouldn't even give his own sister a kiss.'

The old woman nodded her agreement, exchanged a few more words and then took my hand to leave. I turned and waved to my sister, happy to have met her.

That evening before saying the Rosary and going to bed I went out into the back garden of my aunt's house. Overgrown blackberry bushes stooped under the weight of fruit and the air smelled sweet. Having eaten some berries, I reached cautiously through a gooseberry bush and plucked some of its fruit, and though they were not quite ripe I ate them. The bitterness reminded me of Mr O'Rourke and the garden at St Michael's. I rolled the fruits around my mouth, enjoying their taste and the feel of their hairy texture on my tongue.

The raspberries were less difficult to get at. I picked a handful and ate them. I loved the garden, its smells and the long uncut grass rubbing against my leg where my stocking had slipped down. I lay down for a few minutes munching a blade of grass and allowing my nose to be tickled by it which made me sneeze. My aunt knocked on the kitchen window with her ring and beckoned me to come inside.

'Will you look at the state of you,' she said and took me into the kitchen to clean my face, particularly around my mouth.

'You couldn't say the Rosary with a face like that,' she said.

During the night I woke with a violent pain in my stomach. I was desperate to go to the toilet, but was afraid to get out of bed in the darkness of the house. Then I remembered the chamber pot beneath the bed which my aunt told me to use if I needed to go to the toilet during the night. I groped around until I found it, raised the shirt I was wearing and sat on the pot. My bowels emptied hurriedly and I missed the pot almost completely. The pain was intense but I could not shout for help. When it passed I stood up to try and see the extent of the mess. I could feel my feet wet from the faeces on the carpet, and when I lifted the pot up my hands were soiled from dirt on its outside. The smell in the room was almost unbearable, a sour sickening stench. I wanted to go to the bathroom to clean myself before my aunt discovered what had happened, but decided to wait until morning and try to get up before she did. I slept erratically that night, waking and looking towards the window for any sign of morning.

'Jesus, Mary and Saint Joseph,' my aunt shouted. 'What is that awful smell?'

I was startled out of the sleep I had never intended to go into by her shrill voice.

'Have you dirtied the bed?' she asked.

'Just a bit,' I said, explaining that I had wanted to use the toilet during the night but was afraid of the dark.

'I used the pot under the bed,' I said.

'You stupid child, that pot is for passing water. Get out of the bed.'

When she pulled the curtains open I realized the full extent of the mess I had made. My shirt had dried out and become caked to my skin, the carpet was hard where the faeces had dried into it.

'Oh my Jesus, the carpet, the carpet! How am I going to clean that? I should never have taken you, you dirty thing. Is it any wonder your father and mother couldn't put up with you.'

'I couldn't help it,' I said, 'it came too quick.'

'Get out of this room quick. Take that pot with you, empty it and clean yourself.'

As I carried the pot out of the bedroom, I turned and apologized, offering to clean the carpet.

'Get out of my sight,' she said.

I stood naked in the bathroom washing myself. The door opened and my aunt watched.

'Just wait until I write to Mother Paul and tell her what happened.'

I continued washing, unaware of my nakedness until she reprimanded me. 'It is a sin for a man to be naked in front of a woman, you should have a towel around you.'

My aunt didn't speak at all during breakfast except to tell me that I could not go out onto the avenue to play and that she was getting in touch with my uncle to arrange for me to be brought back to the school as soon as possible.

On Friday evening Ria came to the house to find out if I was sick. I heard her telling my aunt that her mother had asked her to call, since she had not seen me for a couple of days.

'He's going back tomorrow.'

'Tomorrow!' Ria exclaimed. 'He told me he was staying for two weeks.'

'He was but the nuns need him back in the convent to serve at High Mass.' I was afraid my aunt was going to say why I was being sent back and was relieved when she didn't.

'Can he come over to my house later on?' Ria asked.

'We'll see,' she said. 'I'll have to get him cleaned up and make sure that he gets to bed before the long journey. I'll bring him over for a few minutes later on.'

'Thanks, Mrs Boyle,' the girl said, before the door closed. My aunt gave me a stern warning about how I was to behave in the O'Neills' house. I presumed it was all right for me to go and, walking towards the hall door, I opened it.

'Wait,' she said.

She put on her coat and checked again in the mirror to see if her hat was all right. Then she took my hand and led me across the road. Ria's mother and father wondered why I was going home so soon.

'Oh,' she said. 'You know the nuns.'

I sat quietly in one of the soft armchairs in the front room and Ria sat on the arm of it.

'Will you write to me?' she asked.

'I will if I'm let,' I answered. 'I don't know if I would be allowed.' Mr and Mrs O'Neill gave me a glass of lemonade and some biscuits and as my aunt led me out of their house Mr O'Neill handed me a ten shilling note. My aunt suggested that she should mind it for me. It was the last I saw of it.

Back in her house we knelt to say the Rosary and as it was Friday, she said the Five Sorrowful Mysteries: the Agony in the Garden, the Scourging at the Pillar, the Crowning with Thorns, the Carrying of the Cross, and finally, the Crucifixion. When the Rosary was finished she brought me upstairs for a bath. She washed my chest and my back, my arms and legs. Then with the face cloth she rubbed hard between each of my toes. When I protested that she was hurting me she replied that she couldn't send me home dirty.

'Wash between your legs yourself,' she said handing me the flannel. As soon as I stepped out of the bath she wrapped me in a long white towel and dried me quickly. She offered me a drink of milk and a piece of bread before going to bed, and as I went upstairs she reminded me to go to the toilet.

Early next morning my uncle called to collect me. He was alone and, judging by the conversation between my aunt and himself, didn't really want to drive me back to

Waterford. As they talked I got into the car and within minutes I was on my way back to St Michael's.

Before leaving Wexford town, my uncle stopped at one of the larger shops and invited me to pick anything I liked from the shelves stacked with toys and books. I told him that I would like a football.

'And what else?' he asked.

'An annual,' I said.

'Pick whichever one you like,' he said.

I picked a cowboy one and handed it to him. He gave it to the shop assistant who put both items in a bag. On the way out of the shop he bought me a large ice-cream cone which I licked as we walked along the street. Someone bumped into me and the cornet fell onto the footpath and when I was about to retrieve it someone stood in it.

It was mid-afternoon before the car drew up outside the high grey gates of St Michael's. My uncle pushed them but they were locked. He pulled the car halfway onto the pathway and switched off the engine. We both walked to the convent door and he rang the bell. It was answered by one of the nuns who had eaten with us on the day he had called to collect me.

'Mr Furlong,' she said, surprised, 'and Pat.' She showed us into the parlour saying that she would get Mother Paul.

In the centre of the highly polished parquet floor there was a mahogany table with six chairs around it. Everything shone and smelt of wax polish. On the wall over the beautiful ornate white marble mantelpiece was a large gilt-framed picture of a woman dressed in the habit of the Sisters of Mercy. Beneath the picture a brass plate had the words 'Our Foundress'.

'Are ye glad to be back?' my uncle asked, his voice barely audible.

'It's all right.'

'Next year ye can come again, you'll be bigger and maybe you'll enjoy yourself better.'

I nodded.

The door of the parlour swung open and Mother Paul came in to greet my uncle. The vindictive look on her face frightened me.

'I'm awful sorry, Mr Furlong,' she said, 'I had no idea this would happen. I was sure the child wouldn't have been any bother.' She took a letter from her pocket and told him that it was from my aunt. 'It just arrived in this morning's post. The poor woman is distracted, God help her.'

She offered my uncle tea but he declined and, when he noticed I had not got my presents, told Mother Paul that he was just slipping out to the car for a second before heading off. While he was out, Mother Paul glared at me and through clenched teeth told me that I 'was in for it'. 'You are going to be a very sorry lad before I'm finished with you,' she said, and would have continued had my uncle not reappeared. He handed me the bag with the football and the annual, then extended his hand to Mother Paul and said goodbye. As he walked towards the door I heard her apologize to him once again.

'Go over to the assembly hall and give Mother Michael all the news, I'll be over as soon as your uncle is gone,' she said.

Thirty years later, as I sat beside my uncle's hospital bed, I wondered if he could remember that day in 1958 as well as I could. As soon as the old man saw me he began to weep and every time I asked a question about my mother, his sister, or my father he avoided answering, saying simply that I would be all right. The conspiracy of silence had gone on so long that this frail old man would not break it. From whatever tiny answers I could coax from him it is only possible to sketch in the conversation he had with Mother Paul that day.

Mother Paul had questioned him about whether my aunt had said anything about me having nightmares. She told him that they were having a lot of difficulty with me talking constantly about my father's death, but assured him that they were doing everything possible to convince me that the nightmares I was having were nothing more than bad dreams.

My uncle tried to stand up but slumped back into the chair. He buried his wrinkled face in his weather-beaten hands and wept.

'I don't know in the name of God what I'll do when the boy is older,' he said.

She reminded my uncle of the resilience of children and how they eventually forget even the most traumatic events and that in a few years it would be as though nothing had ever happened.

When he was with me in the parlour he had been clutching a brown £5 note. If I am still uncertain about everything that passed between them, I know for certain that as he began the lonely journey back to Wexford it was no longer in his possession.

In the assembly hall I was busy telling the other boys about my shortened holiday. I said that my aunt got sick which was why I had to come back. A small group of us looked through the coloured pictures of the annual. Cowboys on magnificent horses, driving herds of cattle or gunning each other down.

'Is he telling you all about his holiday?' Mother Michael asked.

'I hope he's not telling any lies,' Mother Paul added sarcastically as she arrived. She asked one of the boys what I'd told them.

'He said that his aunt got sick and that was why he had to come back, Mother.'

'I see,' Mother Paul said, her voice becoming more and more icy.

'Your aunt was sick all right. Sick of you! Do the honest thing and tell everyone what really happened.' She grabbed me by the ear and guided me through the boys onto the stage in the assembly hall. Threatening me with her cane, which she brought swinging through the air, she made me tell them everything. When I was finished she hit me across the legs twice or three times.

'I'm not going to give you the cane this time, at least not as much of it as you should get.'

I remembered the last time she promised not to give me the punishment I deserved and worried about what she had in mind.

'I want you to wax and polish the dormitory floor first thing on Monday morning, I would make you do it tomorrow only it's Sunday. You'll start immediately after breakfast. Do you understand?'

'Yes, Mother,' I said.

'I'll take that football and the book too,' she said, stretching out her hand. 'Mark my words, it will be a long time before you see them again.' As I walked down from the stage she said, 'I don't want any more trouble from you, no more raving and ranting about hanging men. I want to see an improvement in your conduct and I also want to see you lifting that foot of yours when you walk. Any more trouble and you can expect to feel the full brunt of the cane.'

I attended Mass next morning but, now that I was no longer allowed to serve, I had little interest in what happened inside the altar rails, though I always gave the impression of being in a state of deep meditation and prayer. I kept my head bowed, not out of reverence, but out of fear of being recognized by the townspeople. I envied the boys who were serving for I always regarded it as the ultimate accolade. Now I was just another one of the orphans. Not all the children inside St Michael's were orphaned, many came from broken homes or domestic situations into which they simply didn't fit. Inside the school there was a clear distinction between those who had parents and those who had not. Those who did have a father or mother alive who was an alcoholic were often berated by the nuns. 'Is it any wonder your poor father took to drinking? The poor man must have been at his wit's end trying to manage you.' I don't know if any of the other children there had parents who had committed the mortal sin of suicide. If there were, then like me, they were probably kept in ignorance.

CHAPTER SEVEN

After breakfast on Monday morning, Mother Paul reminded me I had a job to do, not that I had forgotten. I was allowed help in moving the beds but not polishing the floor. Another boy and myself moved two rows of beds to one side of the dormitory before he left me alone. I got the tin of wax polish and, with a piece of wood that was with it, splattered lumps of wax onto the floor at intervals of a few feet, before spreading the orange-coloured paste with pieces of an old sheet, too worn to be used on a bed and barely adequate for polishing a floor.

Spreading the wax was difficult. First I covered the area and, when I had finished, went back to where I had started and began polishing. It was hard, heavy work, demanding a lot of energy. I used a polishing block which was a large piece of wood, with felt tacked to its base. By pushing this back and forth and leaning heavily on it the floor began to shine. It took me many hours to finish the entire dormitory and by the time I had I was exhausted and sweating heavily. I got help to put the beds back, ensuring they were in a straight line, and sat down on the edge of my own, waiting for Mother Paul to inspect my work. I was dozing when I heard her footsteps and immediately got to my feet, pretending to be fixing the lid firmly on the tin of wax. She walked slowly up and down the dormitory between the rows of beds not lifting her eyes from the floor. I stood and waited for her to complete the inspection, hoping she would find nothing to complain about.

'What is this?' she demanded.

She held her fingers so close to my eyes I had to back away to see properly.

'Dust, Mother,' I answered.

'Why is it there?' she asked sharply.

'I don't know, Mother. I didn't see it, Mother,' I answered.

'If you used the eyes God gave you, you would have seen it. Get the dustpan this minute and clean out that corner properly.'

She stood over me checking and double checking until she was satisfied the floor was clean. I told her that I had missed dinner because I was working.

'It's a pity about you,' she said. Then she pointed to the dormitory door saying that I would go without supper too if I didn't hurry.

It was during the following winter when we were all walking around the schoolyard in the cold under the supervision of Mother Paul and Mother Michael, that they called me over. I listened to them discuss how I was dragging my left foot and heard Mother Paul say I was bright enough to be acting the fool, and her guess was that there was nothing wrong with me at all.

'Walk over to the other side of the yard,' she ordered.

I could feel their eyes on me as I looked down at my foot, trying to ensure it was not turned in. Mother Paul spoke.

'Take him to the bathroom, give him a good washing and see that he has underwear on him. I want to take him to see Doctor Black and God help him if he's acting the fool, just God help him.'

'Why have I to go to the doctor?' I asked nervously.

'Because you refuse to walk properly.'

'I can't help it, Mother, honestly,' I pleaded.

Mother Michael ran the bath while I undressed slowly.

'Hurry up,' she demanded.

There was a lot of steam coming off the water and before getting into it I told her it was too hot.

'In the name of God, child, how do you know when you haven't put a finger into it?'

The unfamiliar steam rising from the water scared me. I put one leg over the edge so that just the tips of my toes touched the water, withdrew it quickly and told Mother Michael again that the water was too hot. She took no notice. Using all her strength, she pressed me down until I was up to my armpits in it.

'It's burning me,' I screamed.

She hit me with a wet flannel across the back of the head and told me to be quiet. Only when I persisted crying did she eventually run cold water into the bath, stirring it with circular sweeping movements of her arm. She scrubbed my back with carbolic soap and a rough piece of cloth. I stood up in the bath to allow her to wash my legs. She lost her temper with me when I said that she was hurting me and hit me across the thighs with the cloth. 'You're worse than any two-year-old. Now get out,' she commanded.

She dried me quickly and gave me a white vest and under-pants to wear, all the time urging me to hurry. I was given the suit I wore for my First Communion and a clean pair of socks. She fine-combed my hair with a steel comb which dug into my scalp and when I protested she dug in even harder saying that I probably had a head full of lice.

'Wait here,' Mother Paul ordered, putting her head out the front door to see if the convent car had arrived. Mr O'Rourke was driving. He opened the door and pushed the seat forward to allow me in followed by Mother Paul. The drive was only about two or three minutes and when we got to the house the nun asked the driver to wait. When she wasn't looking the old man winked at me through the open window of the car.

In the doctor's waiting room a man was contentedly puffing his pipe, sending great clouds of smoke towards the low ceiling. When he saw the nun he took off his hat and saluted her, suggesting that she should see the doctor before he did. She accepted the offer and thanked him, before sitting upright in her chair and crossing her hands on her lap. The old man took a newspaper from his coat pocket and unfolded it.

'You don't mind if I read, Mother?' he asked.

'Not at all,' she said.

'I see there's talk of putting dogs into outer space,' he said, 'I wonder what they'll be thinking of next?'

'God only knows,' she replied.

'I just hope they know what they're at,' the man said before relighting his pipe.

The surgery door opened and a woman came out bidding the nun good evening as she walked quickly past.

Mother Paul got to her feet and led me in. The doctor was a white-haired woman in her mid fifties who wore glasses which she carried around her neck on a golden chain. She had a friendly face and gentle voice. She greeted Mother Paul and then looked at me closely.

'I've often seen this little man serving Mass,' she said. 'Isn't that right?'

'Yes,' I replied.

'He's one of the finest altar boys I've seen in the church and a great credit to you. You must be very proud of him, Mother.'

'Indeed we are, doctor,' the nun replied.

The doctor sat down behind her desk and began to write on a sheet of paper, asking the nun my name and age.

'And what is the problem?' she asked, removing her glasses and allowing them to hang from her neck.

'He's walking with his foot turned in, and he seems to be dragging it along the ground,' Mother Paul said.

'When did you first notice this, Mother?'

The nun thought for a minute before replying that she couldn't say for sure, but it had been going on for a good while.

'Can I have a look at your foot, Patrick?' the doctor asked. Her voice was gentle and kind.

It took me some time to undo the laces and I could sense the impatience of the nun as the doctor told me to 'take it easy', before she eventually helped me to undo both boots.

'Which foot is it?' she asked.

'This one,' I said, pointing to the left.

Taking my bare foot in her hand she moved it up and down, then in a circular motion, all the time enquiring whether I was experiencing any pain. She checked the right foot, manipulating it in the same manner, asking if I could feel any soreness or discomfort. During the examination my fear and tension must have been obvious to her because I was being constantly reassured.

'Will you walk down the room and back towards me please, Patrick?' she asked, watching closely as I did so, then asked me to sit on the couch and let my legs hang over the edge to check my reflexes. She tapped my knee gently with her black rubber triangular hammer and the lower part of my leg shot outwards involuntarily. It was a funny sensation and I laughed. With the same instrument she checked my ankles before instructing me to put my boots and socks on again. As I did I listened to her question Mother Paul.

'How is his health generally?' she asked.

'Fine,' the nun replied. 'He eats well and gets plenty of sleep.'

'Is there any history of disability in his family, anything that you think I should know?'

'No.'

The doctor put her glasses on again and looked over the notes she had written. Then told Mother Paul that she could find nothing wrong. I trembled when I heard this because I knew that my punishment would be severe.

'There is the possibility, Mother, that the child is imitating someone with a limp, perhaps his father or mother, and this is his way of bringing attention to himself. I presume his parents are dead if he is in the orphanage?'

'Yes,' the nun said attentively.

'I think the child is suffering some form of trauma and time will put this matter right. It may well be that he needs reassurance and a great deal of kindness. If either of his parents or someone else close to him had a limp it is quite likely he would imitate that, not out of any sense of mockery or anything.'

'I understand,' Mother Paul said.

She asked was I a nervous child and the nun mentioned my fear of dogs.

'Has he had any bad experience with dogs? Has he been bitten or frightened by a dog?'

'Not that I am aware.'

'Does he have nightmares? Has he ever mentioned his parents?'

'No,' the nun replied, 'but we do encourage the children to pray for their parents every night.'

'I see,' the doctor said. There was a brief silence before she spoke again.

'Just one final question. What did the child's parents die from?'

'An accident,' the nun answered.

'A road accident was it?'

'Yes, doctor.'

This story was different from what I had overheard my aunt saying, but again it made little impact on me at the time.

'Thank you very much, Mother, I'd like you to keep a close eye on this little man and bring him back to see me in about a fortnight. We can review the position then.'

The doctor handed me a sweet, wrapped in paper, which she took from the pocket of her white coat. I held it in my hand.

'That's not the place for it, is it?' she asked kindly. 'Are you not going to eat it?'

I undid the wrapper and put the sweet into my mouth, aware that Mother Paul was watching.

'Do you like school?' the doctor asked me.

'Yes,' I replied.

'Are you happy there?'

'Yes.'

She took both my hands in hers and asked me if anyone had ever frightened me, or if I could remember anything terrible ever happening to me. She wondered if anyone had ever beaten or locked me up. I wanted to talk to the doctor, to tell her about the beatings and other punishments given to me by the nuns and about the image of the man hanging that I linked somehow in my mind with my father. I was sure she would believe me but because of the presence of Mother Paul I couldn't speak. Since my parents' death I had been surrounded by a conspiracy of silence. That evening in the doctor's room fear made me an accomplice in it. Looking back I see it as one of the turning points of my life.

Back in St Michael's I played in the yard while the two

nuns discussed what had happened at the doctor's. I remember Mother Paul towering over the smaller figure of Mother Michael as they talked. I can only assume that Mother Michael agreed that she was right in lying to the doctor. They must have realized too, that the caretaker, Tom O'Rourke, limped, and that it was probably him I was imitating. I think they resolved that day to make a greater effort to ensure I would eliminate from my mind the image of a hanged man because any time I mentioned him now I was caned severely. My constant talking of him turned to a frightened silence.

For a week neither of the nuns took their eyes off me. I was constantly reminded to walk properly by a shout or the threat of being beaten.

As I became more aware of being watched I became more tense and my manner of walking grew distinctly awkward. I was constantly conscious of my foot and nervous of being beaten. My limp got worse.

The nuns decided to seek a second opinion and brought me to another doctor. As I walked towards his surgery Mother Paul grabbed me by the back of my jumper and, in a sharp-tempered voice, warned me about walking with my head down, adding that I was bad enough as I was.

The doctor was an elderly man with a red face and a completely bald head. His manner was abrupt and he lacked the sensitivity of the female doctor. After he had enquired from the nun what was wrong with me he made me take off my boots and stockings and walk across the floor.

He enquired whether I had any illness recently and Mother Paul mentioned the measles and the earaches. The doctor spoke to her about polio, reminding her that the country was in the middle of an epidemic of the disease. She assured him that the nuns had warned all the children to keep away from rivers and sewers. The doctor considered for a moment, then told Mother Paul he wanted me admitted to hospital immediately as a precaution. My heart pounded, my breath raced and I could feel tears coming to my eyes. I wanted to plead with him not to send me away, that if he didn't I would do my best to make sure I walked properly.

He wrote a short note which he handed to Mother Paul, instructing her to take me to Cork that evening. Then he telephoned the hospital.

From the doctor's house I was driven back to St Michael's and when we arrived Mother Paul ordered me to stay where I was until she came back. Tom O'Rourke noticed I was crying and he did his best to comfort me by just talking. He took out his pipe and lit it, saying that he didn't like to smoke when the nuns were in the car. As he drew on the pipe I could hear the moisture make a sizzling sound in its stem. After every few pulls he coughed and waved his arm to disperse the smoke.

'I do have to do that,' he said, 'in case the nuns might think the car was on fire.' Then he laughed loudly.

'Begob and d'ye know what it is, I don't think the ould hospital would be all that bad all the same, and sure didn't I hear the nun sayin' that it would be only a week before I'd be going to collect you to bring you back.' I looked deep into the jaundiced eyes of the old man and through my own tears could see he didn't really believe what he was saying. I sobbed and still he tried to comfort me. He looked out the car window to see if Mother Paul was coming.

'Begob they must be having a party in there, she's a good while gone now.'

I drew a deep breath in an effort to stop myself crying and asked him how far away Cork was. He thought for a minute before answering.

'Well I suppose it'll be around the seventy or eighty mile mark,' he answered. 'Sure it could happen that I wouldn't be able to find the hospital at all and then we'd have to come back.'

'How long will it take us to get there?' I asked.

'Three or four hours,' he answered as he looked at his watch. It was getting dark and rain began to fall in tiny droplets on the windscreen. I saw the convent door open and the figure of Mother Paul come out into the grey evening light. Tom O'Rourke noticed her too and pressed his thumb into the bowl of his pipe and put it into his breast pocket then waved his hand towards the open window, urging the smoke to go out.

'Whist,' he said, 'I see herself coming and she has company with her for the prayers. You'd think I was going to kill them on the road.' He got out and opened the door. Mother Paul sat in the back seat beside me while the other nun took the passenger seat. As soon as we moved away, the nun in the front began to say the Rosary. Mother Paul responded and encouraged me to join in. I did make an effort, but the sorrow I felt at being taken away from St Michael's would not allow me to.

As it got dark the lights of oncoming cars dazzled me, and the heavy rain made it difficult to see out. The wipers swished from side to side, but the rain was so heavy, they were of little use in keeping the windscreen clear. Halfway through a Hail Mary Mother Paul nudged me in the ribs.

'What are you crying for?' she asked.

'I don't want to go to hospital,' I answered.

'Don't be stupid, thousands of children your age go into hospital every day of the week – most of them much worse off than you are. You should be thanking God that your complaint is just a simple one that will take no time to put right. Now join in the prayers.'

I did my best to join the nuns as they went from one decade of the Rosary to the next and on to the Litany of Saints. Only when the car stopped and they got out to go into a big store did the prayers stop. When they got back in and the engine started they resumed praying.

Coming into Cork city I was amazed by the different colours of lights flashing on advertising boards, particularly by an advertisement for Donnelly's Sausages, a neon Don tossing a neon sausage to a neon Nelly. Reading the advertisements and listening to the lilting voices of newspaper sellers distracted me from what was happening and I stopped crying. I had never been outside the Industrial School after dark except to go to the local church to serve at Benediction when the missionary priests were conducting their annual retreat for the local people. Now I was in a city, buses, cars and people. Brightly lit streets and illuminated shop windows with shop models dressed in the latest fashions. Despite the noise of traffic, the voices of the newspaper sellers could be heard through the streets urging people to buy an evening paper.

'Would ye mind if I stopped for a minute, Mother?' Tom O'Rourke asked. 'I just want to go into one of the shops to get something.'

'You won't be too long, Tom, will you?' Mother Paul said.

He pulled the car in to the edge of the pavement and limped into a shop that had its window and interior brightly lit. I could see him talking to the shop assistant, indicating with his finger that he wanted something from one of the high shelves behind the counter. The girl stood on a small step-ladder and took down a large box which she handed to him. He looked at it for a few seconds before handing it back to her to be wrapped. When he came out of the shop he was carrying a parcel wrapped in brown paper which he put into the car behind his seat and in front of me. He got in and remarked that 'the next problem would be to find the hospital.' He laughed, the nuns didn't.

The Morris Minor stopped outside a red-bricked building with tall Georgian type windows. Light was shining from each of them. A light over the front door shone onto a large brass plate with the words 'Mercy Hospital' etched onto it. Mother Paul stepped from the car and coaxed me out. I hesitated, but eventually followed her.

Going up the rain-soaked steps to the entrance of the hospital, I stopped and pleaded with her not to allow them to keep me in but to bring me back to the other boys. Embarrassed by the commotion I was causing she grabbed me firmly by the arm and tried to force me up the steps. I stood absolutely still and I would have run but for the tightness of her grip. Her lips puckered as she became annoyed but it didn't worry me. I knew she couldn't hit me now.

'You are only going to have to stay a couple of days,' she said, stressing each word.

'I don't want to go in there,' I screamed.

'In one week, maybe even less, you'll be coming home to us again,' she promised.

Because I believed that nuns never told lies, I stopped crying and walked slowly up the steps with her holding my arm.

A bespectacled, sharp-featured lady took details from Mother Paul before ringing for a nurse to take me to one of the wards. As she arrived I held onto the nun's black habit and pleaded with her not to leave me there. My knuckles were white as she tried to prise my fingers loose. The nurse bent down to try and lift me into her arms.

'No,' I screamed as loud as I could. 'I don't want to stay here, I want to go home. I don't like this place.'

As the nurse tried to talk to me I shook my head violently

from side to side, screaming at her to 'go away', but she persisted and eventually succeeded in lifting me into her arms, telling Mother Paul that I would settle in once she was gone. I watched as the nun opened the main door to walk out. As she did so, Tom O'Rourke walked quickly past her, carrying the parcel he had earlier bought and came towards me. He gave me the present, telling me it would pass the time. I dropped it and put my arms out to him, begging him to take me back to St Michael's with him. Looking him straight in the face, I realized that I loved this man, like a son would love his father. He held my hand tightly in his, and told me that he would probably be staying in Cork for the night because it was too late to return to Waterford. He would be back first thing in the morning to check with the doctors if I could go back with him.

'I want you to be a good lad, I'll be praying for ye and the minute I get the word I will be here to collect ye.'

I was greatly reassured by his words and calmed down considerably. He looked sad as he released my hand, and though I was no longer screaming I still wept uncontrollably. He walked away and stood for a moment at the door with Mother Paul at his side. They waved to me and the nurse tried to get me to wave back, but I couldn't. The heavy doors closed behind them, I shouted after them a last time not to leave me. They did, and though I couldn't have known it at the time and, more importantly, though I was still legally in the nuns' care for the next seven years, I was never to see either of them again nor was I to return to St Michael's School.

A nurse carried me into a ward of about twenty beds. A nun followed dressed in a white habit of the same design as the black ones I had become so used to at St Michael's. In the brightly lit ward I noticed a smell of disinfectant and the chesty coughing of old men, most of whom were watching me curiously. I stood beside my bed waiting for the nurse to get screens so that she could undress me. The castors of the screens made a rattling sound as they were wheeled across the wooden floor. There was a metallic tapping as one section of the tubular steel frame hit against the next. The nun looked crossly at the nurse and said something to her which I could not quite hear. With my view of the ward blocked by the floral-patterned screens I got undressed and, with help from the nurse, got into a new pair of pyjamas Mother Paul had bought specifically because I was going into hospital. Once I was in bed the screens were taken away and the bedcovers tightly tucked in. The coughing of old men surrounded me like a besieging army.

CHAPTER EIGHT

After the nurse left I sat up and looked around the ward. Some of the old men slept with their mouths open and snored heavily, others were busy reading their newspapers and smoking cigarettes or pipes. As they smoked, they coughed and spat into stainless steel mugs on top of their bedside lockers, oblivious to the sickening effect it was having on me.

Meals were being served by three girls in deep pink striped uniforms with white starched caps. They pushed trollies laden with trays each of which had a cup and saucer, a plate and an egg cup. In a rotation system they went around the beds, the first pouring tea, the second bringing milk and sugar and the third carrying buttered bread and a boiled egg. Only by watching the other patients did I know how to manage the egg because I never had one from the shell before.

After the meal one of the nurses went around and asked the patients whether they wanted a bedpan or a bottle. The ones who needed bedpans quickly had their beds screened off while those who wanted a bottle were handed stainless steel receptacles that looked like wine jugs I had seen in a picture bible. I had no idea how to use a bed bottle and when I was offered one I refused, though I did want to go to the toilet. The air filled with the stench of bowel movements and strong urine and took a long time to clear.

As the patients were beginning to settle down for the night and the ward lights had been switched off, I heard the low murmur of a male voice. A doctor stood at the end of my bed, his white coat open and a stethoscope hanging from his neck.

'Is this the boy?' he asked the nurse.

'Yes, doctor,' she answered.

He asked that screens be brought to the bed as he held my wrist to take my pulse, glancing occasionally at his watch until he was satisfied that sufficient time had elapsed, before letting go my hand and moving to the end of my bed to write something on a chart that hung there.

Without warning he threw back the bedcovers and, with the assistance of the nurse, removed my pyjamas so that I was completely naked. I was cold, embarrassed and very nervous as his hands probed various parts of my body in search of any area that was sore. He first tapped my chest with his fingers asking me to say 'ninety-nine'. I felt stupid when he asked me to continue repeating this as he tapped on my back. Through his stethoscope he listened to my chest and back, asking me to take deep breaths, hold them and let them out slowly. Next he checked all my reflex points, never speaking as each of my limbs jumped involuntarily at the very light impact of his triangular rubber hammer. He pressed the glands around my throat and under my arms enquiring if I was feeling any soreness, then checked between my legs for swelling which would indicate the presence of infection. He rotated each of my feet and, asking me to relax, moved them up and down, before holding them firmly and asking me to push against him. After each check, he wrote on my chart.

'Do you feel sore anywhere?' he asked.

'Just a little bit here,' I said, pointing to my stomach.

As soon as his hand pressed on my abdomen I squirmed in discomfort.

'Have you been to the toilet lately?' he asked.

'Before I left St Michael's,' I answered.

He cast his eyes upward and asked the nurse to bring a bottle to me before leaving. I looked down on my nakedness and at the screens surrounding me and wished I could have been polishing boots in the Industrial School.

I was crying when the screen squeaked open and the nurse returned, carrying a stainless steel bottle covered with a cloth.

'I want you to use this for me,' she said and handed me the bottle. I looked from her to it and wondered what I was supposed to do.

'Have you ever used one of these before?' she asked.

'No,' I answered.

'Put it down between your legs and pass water into it.'

When I did get to put the bottle between my bare legs it was freezing cold. I shivered and though I managed to get my penis into it, I could not relax enough to use it. When she realized nothing was happening, the nurse became impatient and raised her voice slightly.

'Concentrate hard on what you are supposed to be doing,' she said.

Eventually I began to urinate, at first only in a trickle but then more forcefully as I relaxed. My penis slipped from the bottle and soaked the bed despite my own best efforts to control it. She grabbed it and stuck it quickly back into the bottle, annoyed that she would have to change the sheets and, as she left to get dry ones, told me to put my pyjamas back on.

She remade the bed and tucked me in tightly suggesting

that I get off to sleep after my long journey. 'You'll be feeling much better in the morning,' she said as she took away the screens. She noticed I was crying and had taken my arms out from under the covers to cross them on my chest.

'What's the matter?' she asked.

'I don't want to go to sleep with my hands under the covers,' I answered.

'Why not?'

'Because the nuns said it was a sin.'

She smiled and told me that she always slept with her hands under her bedclothes and never committed a sin.

'What other nonsense did those nuns tell you?' she asked.

'They said I had to sleep with my hands crossed, because I might die while I was asleep.'

'Put your hands under the covers. I promise you won't commit a sin, and you definitely won't die. Everyone sleeps with their hands inside the bedclothes and they're not dead, are they?' she said, smiling.

'No,' I replied, as she tucked me in again. I kept my hands covered until I was sure she was gone. Then I took them out and crossed them as I had done for so many nights of my life. Eventually I went to sleep.

On the first morning of my stay in Cork breakfast was served early and immediately afterwards the nurses began to rush about tidying beds. Some patients complained that they only had a few hours sleep. One man who was particularly contrary remarked: 'You'd swear it was the Pope of Rome himself that was coming.'

'Now, Mr O'Brien, there's no need for that,' a nurse said good-humouredly.

'Consultants be damned,' the patient retorted.

'You'd be in a bit of a mess if there weren't any.'

'Bejasus, I wonder about that,' he said acidly.

'Watch the language, Mr O'Brien. We have a young child in the ward now.'

He grunted and turned on his side in an attempt to ignore what was happening.

The bustle that went on before a consultant visited a ward was something that I was to become used to as my time in hospital progressed. Floors were swept, ashtrays removed from bedside locker tops and cleaned. Every bed was freshly made up so that it would be easy to turn back the covers should the doctor require it. Charts, medical notes and x-rays were left on bedtables, carefully positioned at the foot of each bed. Outside the ward I heard the shuffling of feet and the muffled sound of voices. A senior nurse opened the doors and a tall good-looking man in his mid fifties came in followed by a group of about twelve students. I watched as he walked around the beds, his voice deep and loud as he enquired from a patient about his health, then muted slightly as he discussed something with the nurse in charge of the ward.

The consultant and his students came to my bedside. He asked the nurse when I had been admitted and where I had come from and read the letter of referral brought to the hospital by Mother Paul. Then he invited one of the students to examine me and offer a diagnosis. The other students formed a semicircle with the consultant behind them, watching closely. My pyjamas were removed and the student checked my reflexes, pulse and breathing. He took a pin from the lapel of his white coat and told me to close my eyes. As he touched me with it, I had to say whether he was using the pointed or the blunt end. Next, I had to stretch out each arm and, with my eyes shut, bring my index finger to touch the tip of my nose. He asked which was 'the bad foot' then took a bunch of keys from his pocket and dragged one of them along my left sole, causing my toes to turn down.

'Do you have any pain?' he asked.

'No,' I said.

'Do you remember ever twisting your foot while playing?'

'No.'

'Did you ever have a bad fall?'

'No.'

'What about pins and needles, did you ever have them?'

'No,' I answered again.

The consultant came to the bedside and squeezed the calf muscles of each leg, before asking his student for a diagnosis.

I vividly recall him saying 'Post Polio'. The consultant and the students discussed whether the diagnosis was accurate, and though there appeared to be some disagreement among them initially, the consultant agreed with the student. He did say it was nothing serious, and that physiotherapy would help. Before moving away he said he expected I would be able to go home within a month. A nurse helped me back into my pyjamas, and remade my bed. Though I was not being allowed home at once, I was comforted by the fact that I would be out of the hospital within four weeks, having no reason to doubt the word of a doctor.

I unwrapped the parcel Tom O'Rourke had given me. It was a jigsaw of over a thousand pieces. The picture on the box was of a tall ship sailing through enormous waves with its sails fully blown. One of the nurses brought me a table which she felt would be big enough to accommodate its size. I opened the box and spilled all the pieces out, fumbling through them for any two that would fit together. I was becoming frustrated and was just about to put it all back in its box, when another nurse offered to help. First, she said, I should find all the pieces with a straight edge, and demonstrated what she meant. Then when I had all these together I could start to make up the jigsaw.

I did as she said and was delighted when I had a string of more than ten pieces. Whenever any of the staff had time they would add a few more pieces, until eventually the picture began to form. The blue and white of the clouds, and the deeper blue of the sea. Huge foaming waves beating off the side of the ship. Working for hours each day on the jigsaw passed the time, and after three weeks it was eventually finished. I was proud of it and took great care to ensure it would not be accidentally broken. Staff who helped boasted about the part they played in its assembly.

It was at night that I missed St Michael's most. I missed the sounds of the other children sleeping, the jangle of the nuns' bell ringing to get me out of bed to use the pot. The sounds in the ward were totally different to what I had been used to. Eerie groans of men in pain or snoring loudly. The familiar red glow from the perpetually burning bulb at the feet of the Sacred Heart statue was replaced by a cold white fluorescent light shining through the glass partition between the corridor and the ward. When I could not sleep I prayed. Not the prayers I had been taught in Industrial School, but prayers I made up. I begged God to make me better so I could leave hospital, promising that I would never sin again if he granted my prayer. Because I had associated hospital with death I also begged to be allowed to live. The first thing I did every morning was to thank God for not allowing me to die during the night.

I hated Sundays in hospital. They began with the night nurses waking the patients very early to prepare them for receiving holy communion. Beds had to be made, patients washed and shaved. Anything on top of a locker was either removed from the ward altogether or placed inside it. Despite protests from some of the men, old newspapers were thrown out. A nun prayed loudly, as she moved up and down the ward, prodding anyone who appeared to be drifting off to sleep. 'Lord Jesus,' she intoned, in a manner designed more to keep people awake than to pray, 'make us worthy to receive you.' Despite this, it was not unusual for someone to snore loudly during prayers, a source of embarrassment to the nun and the man who had to be woken by her. The arrival of the priest was heralded by the gentle ringing of a bell carried by a nun who walked some twenty or thirty feet ahead of him. Again anyone verging on sleep was quickly woken to take communion.

After breakfast, silence had to be maintained as the patients waited for Mass to be broadcast on Radio Eireann. The voice of a priest came from a large wooden radio on a shelf in a corner of the ward. Many of the men fixed their eyes on its illuminated circular dial as the priest reminded his listeners that the Mass they were about to hear was for those who were sick in hospital, and for those who through no fault of their own, could not attend church for the Holy Sacrifice. They took well-worn black-covered missals from their bedside lockers and followed the Mass reverently. On one occasion, I remember someone turned on the radio thinking they were listening to Mass. It was a Protestant service being broadcast on the BBC, at which the nun in charge took great exception, saying that we shouldn't be listening to it at all before abruptly turning it off.

For an hour in the afternoon relatives and friends of the patients came to visit them. Nearly all carried paper bags filled with fruit or biscuits, as well as Lucozade or orange to drink. I watched the visitors and often eavesdropped on their conversations. Children were strictly forbidden to enter the wards as visitors, they had to wait down in the hall or out in a car. It was not unusual to see a man in bed pleading with the sister in charge to allow his sons or daughters in to see him. Rules were rules, and such demands were very seldom granted. Some people took a chance on 'smuggling' children in to see their fathers or grandfathers. Once caught, they were ushered from the ward by an orderly. Wives dutifully went through their husbands' bedside lockers, removing fruit that was beginning to rot. Pyjamas for washing were taken away and replaced by freshly ironed ones, and a check was made on the toilet bags to ensure there was enough soap and sharp razor blades. The absence of visitors around my bed aroused curiosity among the patients and their visitors. They would come and talk to me, bringing a bar of chocolate or a packet of crisps before they enquired where I was from and what I was in the hospital for.

'It's a long way for your poor mother and father to have to come,' one lady said.

'They're dead,' I said, not realizing the impact it would have on her. After a momentary silence she asked me where I lived.

'In an Industrial School.'

She left my bedside and returned to the person she had come to visit. I knew they were talking about me because they stared in unison, with shocked expressions. When they noticed me looking at them, they smiled and I smiled back. Whenever people asked what had happened to me, I told them confidently that I had Post Polio.

'Are you getting better?' they would ask.

'Yes,' I always replied, though I was unsure if I was or not. Their advice was always the same.

'Don't forget to say your prayers and remember that God is good.'

The end of visiting hour was signalled by a nurse walking

through the ward ringing a heavy brass bell and smiling at people as she told them politely that 'time was up'. Many took no notice until a more senior nurse came in and virtually ordered them out. Gradually they left. I often saw a weeping wife holding on to her husband's hand for as long as she could, wondering out loud when would he be 'right'. As she'd leave she'd pull a white handkerchief from her coat pocket and wipe her eyes, her sorrow infectious. Her husband's eyes would also fill with tears as he urged her to go with a wave of his hand.

During my third week in hospital, I wrote to Mother Paul and told her I was looking forward to coming home. I asked her to tell all the boys that I was asking for them and mentioned that I was praying for her and the other nuns every night and looking forward to seeing them all again soon. One of the nurses posted the letter for me and every morning when the letters were given out to the other patients on the ward I waited for a reply. None ever came.

Three weeks became four and I had settled into the routine of the hospital. I became accustomed to bedpans and bottles and had even grown used to the doctors as they went on their 'rounds', although I did worry that one day they might decide to do surgery on me. The idea of having an operation terrified me, and I hoped I would never be taken to theatre. Too often I had seen screens being drawn around a bed or a 'fasting' sign hung up. Whenever there was someone for an operation, an air of tension gripped the ward. A sense of fear among the other patients. The radio was turned down so low it was almost impossible to hear. There was a sense of urgency in the manner the nurses came and went from behind the cordoned-off bed. No sooner had someone been told that they were being 'taken down', than a nun rushed to his bedside wondering if he would like the hospital chaplain to hear his confession. I never knew anyone who refused. As I grew older in hospital, I came to know these nuns as the God Squad.

Despite intensive physiotherapy there was no real improvement in the way I walked. When the consultant asked me to walk across the ward after four weeks I did my utmost to get my foot into its proper position. He expressed openly his disappointment at the failure of the exercises he had been so confident of bringing success, and looked at me apologetically before writing a short note which the ward sister put into an envelope.

Later that day when a nurse came to my bedside and told me to get dressed, I sensed something was about to happen. I wanted to be told that I was going back to St Michael's but my instincts told me otherwise. A nun approached me as I sat dressed on a wooden chair beside the bed and remarked on how nice I looked in my suit. I wanted to ask where I was going and yet didn't want to know. She smiled broadly and told me that I was being sent to a hospital nearer the school.

I immediately broke down and in desperation asked why I had to be moved. I had settled into the hospital. It had taken the place of St Michael's in my life. I was becoming used to its routine, its sounds and its smells. It had become my home. As I wept the nun tried to persuade me I would be much happier, before telling me that I would only be in the other hospital for a week. When I asked what would happen if my foot didn't get better then, she replied confidently that it would.

For the first time in almost four weeks I walked with my boots and socks on. I went to the table where my jigsaw had been since it was completed. I began to take it apart, first piece by piece, then in bigger chunks, before eventually scooping the remainder into its box. Then I put the box into a bag given to me by one of the patients. I sat by my bed waiting for the ambulance to arrive.

In the heat of the ward my grey suit was too warm and my black boots felt heavy and tight on my feet. I opened the laces and did not tie them again until it was time to leave.

An elderly woman wearing a heavy blue cape with red straps criss-crossed over the front of her striped uniform entered the ward and spoke to the nurse on duty. They both walked to where I was seated and the nurse handed her a paper bag containing my pyjamas and toiletries.

'What about his chart?' the older woman asked.

The nurse had forgotten it and followed us down to the ambulance with the record of my stay in the Mercy Hospital.

I began my journey in the ambulance seated on what appeared to be a stretcher. The small panes of frosted glass allowed little light in and the air was still and stuffy. An opaque sliding glass panel separated the interior of the ambulance from the driver and there were two small windows in the back with a red letter 'A' stencilled to them. The elderly nurse sat opposite me and tapped on the window behind the driver to start up. It was not possible to see through the windows and the only sense of movement was the motion of the ambulance over the rough road. Not long into the journey I began to feel sick and told her so.

'Take some deep breaths,' she said.

I did. But to no avail. As I retched and began to vomit, she banged on the glass shouting at the driver to stop. She stooped under the stretcher to get a bowl and I got sick on her cape. She was furious and referred to me as stupid. When the driver opened the back doors to let me out she shouted at him for not stopping sooner. She stepped out onto the country road, brushing her cape down with a towel she had taken from the ambulance.

'Get out, child,' she said to me, angrily.

As soon as she set foot on the road she made me turn towards the ditch and told me to get sick into it. I became very distressed at being unable to control the vomiting and at being referred to as stupid and silly.

'Take plenty of deep breaths,' she said.

I opened my mouth and sucked in the fresh country air. She hit me across the back of the head.

'You're not supposed to breathe in through your mouth, you eejit,' she said. 'It's in through your nose and out through your mouth.'

She demonstrated what she meant and after a few minutes I felt much better though I was shivering from the cold.

'I have a good mind to belt him again,' she said to the driver, 'just look at the state of me and he's no better. How are we supposed to put up with this all the way to Waterford? Are you finished?' she asked me.

'I think so,' I said.

'You better be sure, because I don't want a repeat of this episode.'

Just fifteen minutes after we resumed the journey I was vomiting again and the nurse was shouting to the driver. He stopped immediately and rushed to the back doors. I was dragged from the ambulance and held with my head bent over a low wall.

'Jesus in Heaven,' she said, 'what in the name of God is wrong with this lad that he can't go more than a few yards without throwing up all over the place?'

'Maybe he'd be better in the front with me, it's not as stuffy and he would have something to look out at. That would keep him occupied and maybe prevent him being sick.'

'You know well,' she said to the driver, 'that I am not allowed to have patients in the front.'

'Well, please yourself,' he retorted. 'But it's either that or carry on as we are.'

When the journey resumed, I was put into the front of the ambulance with the driver and nurse. He had the window open and the fresh air made me feel a lot better than I had in the back. I was able to see the fields and the houses in the small villages we sped through. The hedges on either side of the road rushed by occasionally giving way to flat green fields where cattle grazed. In the distance I could see the spire of a church and I asked the driver where it was.

'It's beside the hospital that we have to get to,' he answered, the nurse adding that it wasn't a minute too soon. As the ambulance drove through the town, it appeared to me that everyone was staring at me through the windscreen. I felt as if I was doing something wrong.

The hospital in Waterford was clearly visible from the town. Its stony grey colour and shape stood drearily against the half light of evening, and its large black-barred windows gave it the appearance of a prison. Hurriedly, the nurse got me out of the ambulance and left me at the admissions section of the hospital without even saying goodbye. Inside, the hospital was as drab and dreary as it appeared from outside. The corridors were high, narrow and dimly lit. Ancient people sat in rows on wooden benches along the sides of the corridors, many of them muttering to themselves while others rocked back and forth in their chairs, totally oblivious to anything happening around them. A few shouted obscenities at passing nurses who didn't take the slightest notice. But it was the appearances of these old people that frightened me most. They held cigarettes between feeble, gnarled fingers and, when they inhaled, coughed weak chesty coughs. Some sat slumped in chairs, their heads to one side and their mouths wide open, revealing toothless gums. The only evidence of life was a continuous dribble onto their dark brown dressing gowns.

A nurse came to take me to the ward, and as she took my hand, I protested, saying I didn't want to stay in the hospital. She ignored me and led me into a ward of ten beds. All the patients there were over sixty and probably much older. Like those I had seen on the benches of the corridors some coughed, some slept and others spoke out loud to no-one in particular. Most of them were unshaven and looked dirty. One man smiled at me, saying that I was the youngest old man he had ever seen, before he broke down into a horrible chesty laugh that I was frightened by.

The nurse gave me a pair of oversized pyjamas but I didn't protest. She rolled up the sleeves and the legs until she was satisfied that they were a reasonable fit. Then she folded my own clothes and told me that she was going to put them away in a locker until I needed them again. I asked her when that would be, seeking reassurance that I would not be kept too long in this geriatric environment, but she didn't reply.

Beside me an unshaven man complained bitterly about the pain he was in and wished aloud for God to take him. When he wasn't praying for deliverance he used to talk to me about when he was my age, all the running, the jumping and the climbing of trees. He looked sad and pathetic there, barely able to breathe and unable to sit up in bed without the aid of many pillows pushed under his back and sometimes two or three nurses to hold him.

'Where is it ye hail from?' he asked and became impatient when I didn't answer immediately.

'What part of the country are ye from?' he asked again.

'Cappoquin,' I answered.

'I know it well, I used to sell cattle at the market there

and many's the pig I brought to the bacon factory. What about the big school that's there? D'ye know that?'

'I live there,' I said.

'All belonging to ye must be dead so, are they?'

'I have an uncle and he lives in Wexford.'

'What part?'

'I don't really know.'

'What was it they died from?' he asked.

'A car crash,' I answered.

'It's not so bad when ye have someone all the same. Will ye be in long?' he asked.

'They told me I'd be staying a week.'

He laughed. 'That's what they told me twelve months ago when I came in and there isn't a sight of me getting out.'

Then he sighed deeply and turned his head away saying that the only way he would get out of hospital would be feet first, 'in a wooden suit'.

It was difficult to sleep at night. The coughing, the ravings of a man out of his mind or the sound of a priest imparting the last rites broke the stillness. It was the regularity of death in the hospital which had the most profound and frightening effect on me. I spent a week there, and during it I experienced what death meant for the first time in my life. In seven days, five or six people died. The ritual became familiar, silence in the ward, the radio turned off, the deep voice of a priest invoking God's blessing on the soul of the dead person and a plea to God that he would see fit to take that patient, who had suffered in pain, to his right hand in Heaven where he would live for ever and ever.

Once the corpse had been taken from the ward the other beds were shifted around. The men joked with whoever was nearest the door, that it was their turn next. They referred to it as 'Death's Door'. For some reason I decided that what they were joking about was in fact true and became increasingly worried as I moved closer to the door. I prayed hard remembering the words of the nuns in the dormitory each night before I went to sleep: 'You never know the day or the hour when God will call, and you must always be ready with your soul as white as white can be.' Any black marks would mean eternal damnation.

The way nurses and doctors reacted to death was a source of confusion to me, I could not come to terms with their laughter from behind the screened-off bed, it all seemed so irreverent and disrespectful, and it was not until I was older that I realized that this was to hide how they were really feeling.

While I was frightened by the death of an individual, the men in the ward didn't appear too upset. They joined in the prayers for the soul departed and remained silent until the dead body had been removed from the ward. Once that was done, one of them would pull a bottle of Guinness out of his locker and uncork it while the others gathered around his bed like a bunch of children planning a mischievous deed. In turn they put the neck of the brown bottle to their wrinkled lips and swallowed hard, gasping pleasurably. If a nurse appeared, the bottle quickly disappeared beneath the bedcovers until she was gone. When it was empty they rolled it in as many sheets of newspaper as they could find and left it in a bin at one end of the ward.

In the mornings a man came around the wards selling newspapers and almost all of the men took one from him, even those who looked so frail that it was hard to imagine that they could read at all. They studied the racing page and discussed among themselves the form of the horses and what kind of money they were prepared to bet on them. Heated discussions took place about how good or bad jockeys and horses were. After all the debate the bets were written out on pieces of paper and given to the porter in charge of the ward who would place them when going to the shops to get messages for the patients. When the money for the bets had been added up, a few shillings was added for him as a token of appreciation. In the evening they listened attentively to the radio waiting for the results and, as they came through, marked their newspapers. Those who lost cursed the horse or the jockey, though usually the horse, describing it as a 'three-legged ould nag only fit for the knackers' yard'.

One week after I arrived in St Joseph's I was told to be ready for the ambulance which was to take me to a hospital in Kilkenny. It was another upset in my life but I was becoming used to it, resigned to moving from place to place, not even bothering to ask nurse or doctor whether I was ever going to come back. I shook the hands of each of the patients before I left and they wished me well. As I was saying goodbye to one of the nurses, she told me that the new hospital I was going to would be much nicer than the one I was leaving. There would be children there. As the ambulance doors were being shut she shouted to me to write to her. I said I would, then realized that I didn't know her name. I was sick many times during the journey but the nurse in attendance didn't seem to mind and by the time I reached Kilkenny I was exhausted from retching and vomiting.

The hospital in Kilkenny was of modern design and completely different to any other I had been in previously. It was a single-storey building spread out among the green fields of the countryside. I was admitted and brought down a long glass-walled corridor to the childrens' ward, where I was welcomed by a friendly-faced nurse who took me to a room with just one bed. It had large glass doors looking out across fields towards the spires of Kilkenny city. Once a chart had been made out for me, I was helped to undress and put into bed. The room was quiet and from down the corridor I could hear the voices of the other children shouting and playing. I asked if I would be allowed into the childrens' ward but the nurse said I would have to wait. 'The hospital is new and we have very few patients yet. When things become a bit more organized we will decide what to do with you. How is that?'

'Fine,' I told her.

I found the solitude of the room disturbing and as each day passed and I was not brought into the main ward I became more and more anxious. The only time I was moved was if the weather was fine when the big doors of the room were opened and my bed was pushed out onto the veranda.

During my first weeks in Kilkenny doctors spent a great deal of time examining me, listening to my chest and heart, moving my foot about, testing reflexes and doing the other examinations I had become used to. They asked me many questions, a lot of which, about parents, relations and brothers or sisters, I didn't understand or simply had no answers to. I became frightened that I would be operated on and, with this in mind, always answered in a way which I felt would deter them from taking me to the theatre. I dreaded the idea of being put to sleep, to me it meant certain death.

I found being alone very difficult. I was nine years old and had been used to company for as long as I could remember. Now the days were empty except for the occasional visit of a nurse, a doctor or one of the domestic staff serving meals. The company of sick and dying adults was preferable to the loneliness of my room. The isolation frightened me and convinced me more than ever that I was going to die. It is possible that I was kept separate from the other children because of the stigma attached to being an orphan, or more likely, because of the danger that my condition, as yet undiagnosed, might be contagious.

At night time, the anxiety I felt during the day turned to sheer terror. The image of the hanged man returned to torment and terrorize me. When the fear became unbearable I would scream loudly to get attention and was always greatly relieved by the presence of a nurse, even though their attitudes to me varied greatly. Some tried to find out why I was so frightened and though I wanted to tell them I felt certain they would not believe me. Others became annoyed and demanded that I stop making a racket.

I would turn and twist in bed, trying desperately to get to sleep and away from the fear, but there was no escape, no release. I sweated profusely and often sat up in bed with my knees gripped firmly in my arms. Somehow this position gave me a degree of comfort. To try and sleep I used to kneel in bed and bury my head under the covers with my forehead pressed tightly against my knees. By adopting this position I could muffle my frightened cries and relax my tense body.

Whenever I was found like this I was made to lie down and once I had been tucked tightly into bed I was left alone with the room door slightly ajar. With the silence, the fear returned so that I spent many nights in terror and was always greatly relieved to see the dawn break.

CHAPTER NINE

My nightly terror continued as the weeks dragged on in Kilkenny. Each night out of a deep fear of dying, I begged God's forgiveness for any sins I had committed and prayed fervently for a cure and a return to St Michael's and the nuns. The light from the corridor shone through the mottled glass of the door. Whenever I heard footsteps outside or saw a shadow pass I cried aloud hoping to be heard. I couldn't find a position that was comfortable. Finally when complete exhaustion overcame me I'd scream. I didn't care what the nurses said to me any more, I was too terrified to, and besides even a bad-tempered nurse was better than the image of the hanging man. One night, a month after I arrived, the night nurse came in.

'What's wrong with you?' she asked, trying to hide her irritation.

'I can't sleep,' I sobbed.

'If you're tired you can sleep.'

'I am tired, I am tired, but I can't sleep,' I pleaded.

'Then there must be something wrong with you?' she said, becoming more annoyed.

I wanted desperately to talk to someone who would understand the agony I was enduring and the awful fears that were my constant companions. I wanted her to under-stand the reality of the image I was seeing with increasing regularity. If I could do that she might understand why I was so distressed and anxious. Then I remembered the nuns and how they described what I was seeing as nonsense. Why should a nurse be any different? Because I said nothing which would have led her to understand why I had screamed the nurse told me to stop being ridiculous and to count sheep. I didn't even know what she meant and as she left the room I pressed my face down into the mattress and cried.

Later when she checked and found me still awake and distressed, she returned with a doctor. He placed his hand on my sweating forehead.

'What are you frightened of?' he asked.

'I don't like being on my own,' I said.

He told the nurse that I was hysterical about something and she agreed.

'Has he said anything?' he enquired.

'Nothing.'

He asked again what was frightening me but again I couldn't tell him. He asked the nurse for my chart, wrote on it and told her to give me two Phenobarbitone tablets immediately, and to keep me on that dosage three times a day. Within minutes the nurse returned with a tumbler of water and two capsules which she handed to me. One at a time I put them into my mouth and swallowed them with the aid of a drink.

'Now, I don't want to hear another sound out of you,' she said as she held the bedcovers aloft to allow me to get down under them before tucking me in. 'Off to sleep,' she said, leaving the room and closing the door gently behind her.

It was dinner time next day before I woke. I was groggy

and didn't feel like eating the meal offered to me, but the nurses persisted until eventually I began to eat and as I did so I became more conscious of my surroundings. I felt relaxed, no longer afraid of the room or of dying. The sun shone through the large glass doors, warming the room and its brightness made it difficult for me to open my eyes properly.

When I had finished eating I asked a nurse if I could write a letter adding that I did not have either a pen or paper. She returned with a blue writing pad, matching envelopes and a biro which she said she was lending to me on condition I took good care of it and gave it back when I was finished. I addressed the letter and wrote:

Dear Mother Paul,
I hope you are well as I am myself thank God. I pray for you and all the other nuns every night and I also pray for all the boys.
I would be grateful if you would send me the anual my uncle gave me when I was on holidays as I am in a room on my own and I get lonely for something to do. In case you cannot find the anual, Mother Michael left it on top of the press in the classroom.
I remain,
Yours truly,
Patrick Doyle.

I decided to wait and show the letter to the nurse who had given me the writing materials before putting it in the envelope. She read it quickly and remarked that although there were one or two mistakes, she doubted that anyone would even notice them. Before I could say anything, she had the letter in her pocket with a stamp affixed, ready for posting.

It was nearly a fortnight before a reply came from Mother Paul. Her letter arrived in a brown envelope with a black harp printed on the front. In the bottom left hand corner the words 'St Michael's Industrial School, Cappoquin' were printed in black lettering between two thin black lines. The nurse who had posted my letter stood by the bedside as I opened the envelope. The reply was short.

Dear Pat,

I got your recent letter and I am glad to know that you are praying for us all here. Your writing is not as good as it should be and I expect that it will improve before you write again.

At the moment I am very busy and cannot find the book you asked for. I am disappointed that you could not spell annual right.

Good Bye,

God Bless,

Mother Paul.

I showed the letter to the nurse and I'm certain she said 'bitch' as she read it. It was the last time I was to hear anything from St Michael's Industrial School or from any of the nuns in it, although their legal responsibility for me as ordered by the courts did not end until 19 May 1967.

I had spent a long time, perhaps a year, in a room on my own before I was eventually moved out into a ward with other children. It was a move I had looked forward to, but one I was to deeply regret. This was the period in my life when I felt most alone and came to realize fully the stigma of being orphaned. Some of the children delighted in my never having visitors, and jeered me about being an orphan, and about how my ears stuck out. When I cried they used to throw wet face cloths at me. Isolation was better than almost constant taunting. I'd scream at them to leave me alone, but they continued until a nurse reprimanded them, and told me I was worse to be taking any notice of them.

I hated night time, the drugs I had become dependent on no longer had the effect they used to. Death figured again in my life, and though I didn't actually see any images of a hanged man this time, I was always terrified they would appear and I realized that this fear would be another cause for the children to mock me. I used to sleep hunched in a ball, my knees flexed under me, my head bent down with my forehead resting on them and my face pressed tightly to my thighs to muffle my crying. Nurses repeatedly reminded me that I was nine years old, no different from any other child, and that I should act my age. When I complained about being pelted with wet cloths and called names, they paid little attention. As the dosage of medication I received was increased it became easier to cope with what was happening around me. The price was addiction to drugs, an addiction that would cause me much suffering and take years to overcome.

For an hour every Wednesday the ward was quiet while Hospitals' Requests was on Radio Eireann, with each patient hoping to have a request played for them. When one was played and the names of parents and relatives read out, there was always some jeering. Good-natured banter about the name of a father or an uncle often turned into a vicious row with things being thrown across the ward by two combatants. I remember one boy having a request played from his mother, father, his uncle Dick and aunt Mary, which immediately brought a chorus of: 'Mammy, Daddy, Uncle Dick, went to London on a stick, the stick broke, what a joke, Mammy, Daddy, Uncle Dick.' It was strange events like this that brought a sense of reality to the sterile atmosphere of the hospital. Children would act as they might in normal circumstances, physical barriers such as plaster of Paris on broken arms or fractured legs could not restrain anger or dampen furious tempers. One evening as two boys, both almost completely paralysed, were having a game of chess, one accused the other of cheating. Both had only the slightest use of their arms, and as they threatened to kill each other, they moved their wheelchairs as close together as they could. Then slowly, each managed to get his hand to his head, by using his fingers to make it 'walk' up his body. With a swear, each allowed their paralysed arms to fall, as a dead weight, on the other. There was never the slightest chance of injury being inflicted and the physical effect of receiving a blow was nothing like as exhausting as that of raising a limb.

The chief consultant in the hospital was a small, chubby, sallow-skinned man with steel-grey hair neatly combed in waves back from his forehead. His hands were said to have been blessed by Pope Pius XII. I often heard adults talking of the great healing powers he had in those hands. When he did his 'rounds' and came to my bed I was always afraid, certain that one day he would decide that an operation was the only way to straighten my foot. My nervousness was obvious, I became tense and fidgety, my breath came fast and I sweated a lot. Whenever he examined me he always did his best to relax me. In my early days at that hospital his examinations were never intense, the most he did was to hold my foot in his hand and move it about gently, but as time went on and he became less and less satisfied with my rate of progress, he became more thorough in his effort to discover what could be wrong.

One Thursday, he examined me in a manner he had not done before. He pricked my foot with a pin, asking me to close my eyes and tell him if I could feel its point. He checked my breathing, and made me follow his finger with my eyes as he moved it slowly across my line of vision. 'Good,' he said as I managed all the tests put to me. Then he asked me to stand out on the floor. The parquet wood felt cool beneath my feet and momentarily I was reminded of the times I used to throw off my boots and socks in St Michael's and run across the field that separated the convent from nearby agricultural land. As I stood, he said he was going to push me and I was to do my best not to let him knock me down. With his first push on my chest, I rocked back on my heels and it required the swift movement of a nurse to prevent me falling. I was caught unaware by the suddenness of the move and I said so. Before he attempted the same thing again, he asked if I was ready. I was. Putting both feet firmly on the floor, I hardly moved, except for a slight swaying initially. Back in bed, he asked me to perform tasks I had done before. I experienced no difficulty in doing anything asked of me and the consultant praised me for that. I was so anxious to impress that when he asked me to walk across the ward, I tripped and almost fell. I steadied myself and slowly began to walk across the room looking down at my feet as I went along, each step being taken slowly and deliberately.

'Don't look down at your feet as you walk,' he said as I returned to where he was standing, adding, 'don't be afraid to walk, you won't fall, try moving a bit faster.'

Standing back from the bed he spoke to those around him, junior doctors, nurses and the ward sister. He could find nothing physically wrong, no evidence of paralysis or muscle wastage. Yes, there was a slight inversion of the foot but it was nothing serious as far as he was concerned. He asked the nurse in charge to have me measured for a splint, a steel bar that would be strapped around my leg below the knee and run down the outside of the lower leg into a hole in the heel of a new pair of boots which were also to be ordered. This he hoped would pull my foot outward and eventually rectify the problem. As the consultant wrote on my chart I heard him enquiring about my parents. The most senior nurse pointed to a piece of paper and said that I was a 'Ward of the State'. It was the first time I had been referred to as such. He wondered how my parents died, adding that he presumed they were dead.

He was assured they were, but the circumstances were not altogether clear, though she presumed 'natural causes'. The consultant wondered at what age the deaths occurred and he was given my date of birth and the date I was committed to the Industrial School. He remained silent as the nurse told him that I cried a lot and had great difficulty in getting to sleep at night. When she was asked if I had ever spoken about what was distressing me, she replied that I had not. He then asked what medication I was on.

'Phenobarbitone,' the nurse said, 'it has calmed him a great deal.' He thought for a while, expressed his dislike of Phenobarbitone, but added that if it was helping it should be continued. Before moving away, he requested the nurse to try and obtain whatever information there was on myself and my family. She made a note of it and slipped it into the brown folder containing my medical records. He pinched me gently on the cheek and told me not to worry about anything. 'We'll have you right in no time at all.' I felt confident enough to ask him if I would have to have an operation.

'Why?' he asked.

I hesitated for a moment before telling him I was afraid of operations.

'You don't worry about operations, you won't have to have one.'

I felt so happy that day that I decided to write to my

uncle, telling him I was in hospital and asking him to come and see me or to send something I could play with. If he wasn't able to get a game, I asked him to send some money, saying that I would buy something myself. No sooner had I given the letter to a nurse to post than I was sorry for writing it. My uncle had not been a part of my life since I last saw him on the day he left me back to the school from my aunt's. I worried about him writing to the nuns to tell them I was begging.

I had become particularly friendly with a fat round-faced boy from Kilkenny, whom some of the others called 'Fatso', a name he hated and which caused him to issue the fiercest of threats to those guilty.

'I'll break your fucking neck,' he used to say, 'as soon as I can get out of this plaster.'

He was older than most of the other boys by about two years and was in hospital to have his leg straightened at the knee. He had had surgery and was in plaster of Paris. He liked to read and chew sweets or gum, if he could get it without the nurses knowing. He was an avid radio listener and, with his guitar, used to mimic Cliff Richard or Elvis Presley. Occasionally he tried to play some of the instrumentals which the Shadows had made popular at that time. 'Apache' was his favourite. He hated anyone to touch the instrument, anyone who did was warned that they would end up with their necks in plaster. Somehow, I looked on him as the one person who would take my side when all the others were jeering me, and though he was immobile I was satisfied that he would one day carry out the threats he was issuing from his bed.

'You leave him alone, you little bastard,' he'd say and anyone who was teasing me stopped immediately out of fear of him. I was afraid of him too, and because of that, I never did anything to turn him against me.

I was careful to agree with him when he said that Cliff Richard was better than Elvis Presley, though I hardly knew the difference between the two. He used to buy chewing gum with pictures of various stars in the packet and keep them in his locker in a scrap book. He spent a good deal of time doing his hair to look like Cliff. He had his own large jar of Brylcreem which he applied liberally and with the aid of a double-sided mirror he combed it back with a coiff at the front.

'What's that like?' he'd ask.

'Grand,' I'd reply.

'Is it like that?' he'd say, holding up Cliff's picture.

'Yeah, very like it.'

Then he would pick up his guitar and play the first few chords of 'Travellin' Light' or 'Livin' Doll' before beginning to sing, doing his utmost to sound like his idol.

'When I get out of here,' he said, 'I am going to start a band.'

At night after I had been given my tablets, John Gorman and I used to pull our beds as close together as we could. He had a cage in his bed to keep the weight of the bedcovers off his plastered leg and from the bars of this he'd hang a small transistor radio tuned to Radio Luxembourg. He also had a torch which he hung beside the radio so he could read when the lights had been put off. He was curious to know why I never had visitors. Because I wanted him as a friend I didn't hesitate to answer anything he asked. As I was not exactly sure of how my parents had died, I told him they were killed in a car crash and that I was in the back at the time. It seemed the easiest thing to say and avoided the necessity for further awkward questions. He wanted to know where I lived and who looked after me.

'A school, with a whole lot of other boys. Nuns look after us.'

'I hate nuns,' he said.

I repeated what he said, and then realized that for the first time I was expressing how I really felt about Mother Paul and Mother Michael, finally admitting my real hatred of them to somebody. I was about to ask him what it was like to have parents when we heard a nurse approaching. He turned off the radio and the torch and pretended to be asleep.

Everything was quiet for a while then he whispered to me that his mother and father slept in the same bed. I said I didn't believe him and repeated what my aunt had told me about men being naked in front of women.

'Cross my heart,' he said making the sign of the cross over the pocket of his pyjamas' top.

'Do you know the difference between men and women?' he asked.

'No,' I said.

He made me swear on the bible that if he told me I would not tell anyone else, ever. I promised.

He said that one Sunday morning he had rushed into his parents' bedroom without knocking and his mother was standing on the floor with no clothes on her. He described her breasts as 'diddies' and said that she had no 'mickey' like a man, just a big bunch of hair with a slit in it. His father had roared at him to get out and never to enter the room again without knocking. Then he asked if I knew how babies were made.

'No,' I answered, sensing that there was something wrong with the conversation taking place, and yet wanting to know. Again I had to swear never to tell before he would continue. He said it was a bit dirty and wondered if I really wanted to hear it.

'Yes,' I said.

'You know sometimes,' he said, with a tremble in his

voice and hesitated, 'when your mickey gets hard and stands up?'

'Yes.'

'Well the man puts his mickey up into the woman's bum and pisses into her.'

'How do you know?' I asked.

'I just do,' he replied, before saying that another boy had told him. I was gripped by a strange, inexplicable sensation that made me want to hear more, even though I was feeling guilty as if doing something wrong.

'You can only do it at night,' he said, 'because that's when your mickey gets hardest and that's when you have the most piss saved up inside you.'

He kept silent for a short while and then asked, 'Did you not know that?'

'No,' I replied.

I was becoming sleepy as John Gorman asked me again to keep what he said a secret. I agreed and said I was going to sleep. Without thinking, I put my hands under the covers and was surprised and a little frightened by the pleasure I was getting from feeling my own erect penis.

'There's a letter for you,' a nurse said as she tossed an envelope onto my bed next morning. I was surprised that the envelope was white and knew immediately that it had not come from St Michael's. I opened it and unfolded a single sheet of notepaper, out of which a £10 note fluttered down onto my bedcovers. In my excitement I grabbed the money in case anyone saw it and stuffed it under the mattress before reading the letter from my uncle. He didn't say much except that he was enclosing money and hoped that I would be able to buy whatever I wanted. He signed the letter, 'Uncle Con'.

I couldn't wait to tell John Gorman but before I did, I made him swear not to tell anyone. He suggested that if he said anything about the money I could tell what he told me about babies and the difference between men and women. Slowly and with great caution, I took the money from under my mattress and showed it to him. He gasped and asked who sent it to me.

'My uncle,' I said.

'Jesus,' he responded, 'he must be awful rich.'

'He is,' I said, jumping at the chance to give him a better impression of me. I said that my uncle was living in the house my parents used to live in, that it was a big house and there was a farm with it.

'When I'm twenty-one,' I said, 'I'll be getting it all as well as the money my mother and father left me.'

I don't know how I came out with that tale but it was obvious that John was impressed and, from that day, his attitude to me changed. I even somehow managed to convince myself that there was a house, a farm and money waiting for me. One day, I would be rich.

'Jesus!' Gorman exclaimed again. 'Ten pounds is an awful lot of money, you could buy loads of things with it. All you have to do is hide it until your new boots and splint come, then you can go to the shop and get ice cream and lemonade and sweets and cigarettes.'

'What would we do with cigarettes?' I asked.

'Smoke them of course.'

It was a hospital rule that patients couldn't keep money, it had to be handed up to the sister in charge of the ward. Gorman got annoyed when I told him so, and said that I would be mad to give it up because the most I would get at any one time would be sixpence or a shilling, which he described as being 'fuck all use'.

'Hide it,' he urged.

'What happens if I'm caught?' I asked nervously.

'Nobody is going to know you have it as long as the

two of us keep our mouths shut,' he said.

'Suppose,' I said, 'that someone asks where I got the money when I go to the shop?'

'All you have to do is say you're getting messages for a patient in the men's ward.'

Later, when a nurse came around asking if anyone had money to be 'handed up', I remained silent.

When my splint and boots arrived a nurse fitted them on me. She tied the shining leather boots tightly and then fixed the iron splint firmly to my leg. Before being allowed to stand out of bed, I had to sit for a time with my legs hanging over the edge. As I did, I noticed the tightness of the boots on my feet and in particular the pulling effect of the splint on my foot. Before I stood up, I mentioned that the leather strap just below my left knee was hurting me, and she loosened it slightly. Even though it was extremely uncomfortable I said nothing, fearing I would not be allowed up. I had spent long enough in bed, now I was anxious to be walking again. I looked forward to the freedom. There would be the opportunity to play table tennis and walk around the hospital grounds. But it was the shop I was most excited about. Having money of my own, and being able to spend it was a new experience, one I was determined to enjoy.

I felt desperately weak when I stood up and was certain that I would faint. The blood seemed to drain from me and I could almost feel my face turn white. The nurse looked at me and could see I was in difficulty.

'Are you all right?' she asked.

'Just a bit dizzy,' I answered.

She held my arm as I took a few steps and enquired how I was feeling. I felt less weak, and said so. After two or three minutes walking she suggested that I sit on the bed and only take short walks with long rests in between until I got used to being up. She warned that under no circumstances was I to leave the ward.

'Never?' I asked incredulously.

'Well not today anyway.'

Later that day as I was walking along the corridor with the nurse, the consultant approached and recognized me. He gestured to her that he wanted me to keep walking and, having watched, said that he would like to see me the following week, 'after he has had some time in the caliper.'

As I became stronger my walking improved and I was free to move around the ward and the grounds outside as I wished. John Gorman watched my progress and eventually suggested that I go to the shop. The £10 note which had been hidden for almost three weeks was withdrawn from under the mattress.

'What will I get?' I asked.

'Lucozade, biscuits, twenty "Players" and a box of matches.'

'How am I going to get cigarettes?' I asked.

'Just ask for them.'

'What if I get caught?'

'Say they're for one of the men.'

Nervously, I left the ward and walked up the long corridor to the shop which was situated in a room adjacent to the men's ward. A small group of men had gathered outside it, all in dressing gowns. As they chatted among themselves I stood at the end of the queue and rehearsed over and over in my head what I was going to ask for when my turn came to be served. I wanted to sound confident.

'Are you new here?' one of them asked.

'No. It's just that I was in bed until I got this,' I said, pointing to the splint.

'Now that you're up and around, it won't be too long before you'll be heading home.'

'I don't know,' I answered.

I never expected to find a nun serving in the shop, and if John Gorman knew, he said nothing. She looked to me and asked what I wanted.

I drew a deep breath and quickly told her. I was going to add that they were for one of the men but decided against it. To my surprise she put everything into a brown paper bag, took the money and asked me to wait a minute for the change. I took it, and without checking stuffed it into my trousers' pocket and walked as quickly as I could back to the ward.

Just as I left the bag on John Gorman's bed the sister in charge of the ward appeared, demanding to know what was in the bag and who gave me permission to leave the ward. 'I don't know,' Gorman said, 'Pat Doyle bought them and he was leaving them on my bed because he was tired.'

I glared at him and felt cheated.

She emptied the bag and held the cigarettes aloft. 'I don't suppose,' she said, 'either of you had the slightest notion of smoking these.'

'No, Sister,' I said, and John agreed.

I had thought of telling her they were for one of the men and that I was going to bring them to him later, but I realized she wouldn't believe me. I admitted having bought them for myself and John Gorman. He was furious and denied any knowledge of the cigarettes.

Then the question of where the money came from arose. Because it was such a large amount of money I was convinced she would think I had stolen it.

'I got ten pounds from my uncle in a letter.'

'You know the rules regarding money,' she said.

'Yes, Sister.'

She held her hand out and I dug deep into my pocket

and took out what money I had. She left the ward with it and the messages.

'You're a pig,' I said to Gorman, furious with him.

'Don't call me a fucking pig,' he replied angrily.

'You made a promise and you broke it.'

'Did I say anything about the money?' he said. 'Did I?'

I threatened to tell the ward sister what he told me about babies. He sat upright in bed, pointed his finger, then squinted his eyes and swore to break every bone in my body if I opened my mouth.

'You're a bastard,' he said, after a brief silence.

'I'm not,' I retorted.

'You don't even know what the word means,' he teased.

'I do.'

'What?' he snapped.

When he realized that I hadn't the slightest idea, he grinned and said that I was a bastard because I didn't have any parents. 'That's what a bastard is.'

I walked away from him, realizing that the friendship we had was beginning to crumble and, angry though I was, had no wish for that to happen. It was he who got me through the rough times in the hospital. I had never wanted to be on the receiving end of his anger. Despite my feelings towards him at that moment, I hoped that our relationship would not be ruined.

In time we forgot our quarrel and once John Gorman was allowed out of bed I had a companion with whom I could walk around the hospital grounds. When the weather was fine we used to sit in the fields while he pointed out the direction of various Kilkenny landmarks like Castlecomer coal mines and the steeple of the Cathedral. He could also show me where his house was. At six o'clock most evenings, both of us would go to the shop and spend any money he had been given by relatives the previous day. Anything we bought was carefully concealed as we made our way cautiously back to the ward and headed for the toilets. One evening, while we were both in one of the cubicles, John Gorman sat on the toilet bowl and carefully stood his crutches against the wall. He lit two cigarettes and handed me one. He had smoked before but I hadn't. I watched as he inhaled the smoke deep into his lungs and allowed it to stream out his nostrils. I drew on mine, filling my mouth with smoke, before taking a deep breath. I nearly choked. I could feel the smoke crushing my lungs and as I gasped I felt my face redden and my head become light. The cubicle spun as I coughed uncontrollably and tears streamed down my cheeks.

'Shut up,' Gorman said, 'or you'll get us caught.'

I tried to say something but could only cough. It was some minutes before I got my breath back and the dizziness subsided.

'Pull on it like this,' he said, holding the cigarette between the thumb and first finger with the burning end covered by the cave formation of his hand. He pulled deeply on it and asked me to do the same. I tried but couldn't and when he stood up I threw the half-smoked cigarette into the toilet. I watched it sizzle and become saturated before fragmenting into tiny pieces. I knew I was going to vomit and gestured for Gorman to get out of the way before bending over and being violently ill.

'For Jesus' sake,' he said.

A sudden knocking on the door startled both of us. The familiar voice of the ward sister demanded to know who was in the toilet. I spewed out what was left in my mouth and spat into the bowl to eliminate the sour taste of sickness and tobacco.

'I want both of you out here this minute,' she said.

Slowly John Gorman slid back the chromed bolt of the

toilet door, before putting a crutch under each arm and inching his way out. I followed.

'What happened to you?' she shouted at me.

'I was sick,' I replied.

'I wonder why?' she said sarcastically, asking us both to turn out our pockets. Picking up a packet of cigarettes which had fallen from my pocket she warned that we would get the severest punishment. 'Both of you will go back to your ward, get straight into bed and you will remain there for a week.'

Later that night both our beds were taken from the main ward and moved to the babies' unit. The nurses pushing the beds took no notice whatever of Gorman's threats to get his father after them and that he was going to run away in the middle of the night.

There were fifteen or twenty babies in the ward, often no more than a few weeks old, who cried, demanding to be fed. Some were in plaster from the soles of their feet right up to under their arms. Nurses had difficulty in lifting them from their cots for feeding while others could not be lifted at all. They were on traction with weights on pulleys, hanging from their legs. Those that were being fed sucked contentedly on their bottles. They slept as the nurse changed the pads which had been placed at the cut-outs in the plaster at the backside and the pelvic area. In the soft light of the ward I could see babies with large heads and tiny bodies and others born without limbs or with only part of hands and legs.

As I was drifting to sleep John Gorman threatened to run away and asked if I would go with him. He said he had no intention of spending a week 'stuck in a ward full of squealing babies and shitty nappies'. He swore he would be gone by morning.

I woke early next morning to find Gorman still in his bed,

curled in a bundle beneath the sheets, oblivious to the sounds of babies demanding breakfast.

The ward sister arrived and told me that the doctor was going to see me and she wanted me 'up and out of bed immediately'. I hadn't expected to be allowed up so soon after beginning my punishment and was surprised that the doctor wanted to see me. I sat motionless until she hurried me.

As I got dressed she awoke my companion and told him we were both being given a chance, provided we gave an assurance to stay in our own ward and not to smoke in the future.

I was worried about seeing the consultant, even though I felt sure he would be happy with the progress I was making. I washed my face a couple of times and brushed my teeth until the gums bled. I combed my hair where bits of it stuck up, wet it and combed it down.

'What are you all cleaned up for?' Gorman asked.

'I have to see the doctor,' I replied.

'He'll probably want to take you down,' he jeered.

'He won't,' I said, not really convinced by my own words. 'He already said I wouldn't have to have an operation.'

'They always say that,' he replied, 'and then they change their minds.'

'You think you know everything,' I said, walking away from him.

I was brought to a room off the main ward to await the arrival of the doctor and as I sat there I prayed silently that he would not operate on me. I practised walking, watching my feet and trying to ensure they were straight.

When he arrived he was in a cheerful mood, rubbing his hands together as he asked me to walk across the room. I stood up and took the first few steps cautiously, looking downward all the time. Halfway across the floor my leg flexed at the knee and I had difficulty in getting it back down to the floor again.

When I turned to face him, he asked me to raise my head, and ignore my feet. Again my leg flexed and the harder I tried to get it back down the worse it became, until, in a sudden movement, it released like a string snapping and I walked the rest of the way.

'What happened there?' the consultant asked.

'I don't know,' I said.

'Has that ever happened to you before?'

'Only since I got the splint.'

'And does it happen often?'

'Just when I get afraid.'

'And are you afraid now?' he asked.

'Just a bit.'

'Sit down there.' He pointed to a chair and told the nurses who were with him that he didn't see any further need for the splint. 'It doesn't appear to be doing any good and in fact it may be causing harm.' He asked me to walk without it. My feet felt free and light, there was no difficulty walking and no involuntary flexing.

'Patrick,' he said, 'you've been here for a long time now, nearly two years, and we haven't been able to put your foot right.' I waited anxiously for what was coming next.

'Because you're not getting any better I want to send you to another hospital to see a specialist who will be able to help you. Once that happens you will be able to go back to your school and the friends you have there.'

I began to cry and said that I didn't want to go back to the school and I didn't want to go to any other hospital either.

'It's for your own good,' one of the nurses said.

'I don't care, I like it here and I want to stay.'

The consultant intervened, 'But you don't want to spend the rest of your life in hospital. Do you?'

'No,' I said hesitantly.

'Right then, we'll get this other man to have a look at you, and we'll see what happens from there.'

'Will I have to stay in the other hospital?'

'Just for a little while, until they do some tests. Once they have been done we should be able to get that foot right for you.'

He wrote a letter on a piece of hospital headed notepaper and put it into a long white envelope which he sealed and addressed to 'Professor E. D. Casey, Consultant Neurologist'.

'What does it say on the envelope?' I asked.

He held it up for me to read. I read the name and then stopped.

'Consultant Neurologist,' he said.

'What's a neurologist?' I asked.

'Just another type of doctor, that's all, nothing to worry about.'

CHAPTER TEN

For two days I roamed around the hospital stunned and unable to believe that I had to leave. I had made it my home, I had friends there, I liked the way I was treated and had come to enjoy the companionship of the other boys. The initial stress-filled weeks of being teased and tormented seemed a long time ago and irrelevant now. I wanted to stay. John Gorman tried to be consoling, and said that he would visit me when he went home.

'But it's in Dublin,' I said.

'How do you know?' he asked.

'I heard the nurses saying so.'

'That doesn't matter, I can get my father to take me. Anyway you won't be staying there for long.'

I wanted to agree with him, but I knew I wouldn't see that hospital or John Gorman again. Promises made by nurses and doctors were something I had learned to mistrust. I had heard them all before and things never worked out the way they said they would.

On the day I was leaving, after I had said goodbye to the patients and nurses, the sister in charge took me by the hand and led me from the ward. I cried bitterly, pleading with her not to send me away. I dug my feet into the floor to prevent her dragging me further.

'I'm not going to any new hospital,' I screamed at the top of my voice and as we were nearing the top of the long sloping corridor I gripped a radiator and held it until my knuckles turned white. She pulled at my arm but I was determined not to budge. I kicked out, attempting to catch one of the nurses across the shins and threatened to kill them if they didn't leave me alone. I was so determined not to leave that it took three nurses to make me release my grip on the radiator.

Though my vision was clouded by tears I could see the senior nurse talking to a doctor. I couldn't hear what they were saying and I didn't care. They stopped dragging at me and for a moment I thought I was going to be returned to the ward, then I saw the doctor return. He had a needle and syringe prepared in the kidney dish he was carrying.

'Now, Pat,' he said gently, 'this will make you feel better.'

'I don't want that needle,' I protested.

He inserted the needle into a vein in my right arm which was held in an outright position. I felt it puncture my skin and I screamed again. Within minutes my screaming and protestations stopped, my vision became clouded and my mouth felt dry. I was so light-headed that I could no longer walk. I had to be lifted and carried to a waiting ambulance where I was put lying on one of its two stretchers. The nurse who was travelling woke me when we reached Dublin. I was thirsty and she gave me some water from a plastic bottle.

'How far is it now?' I asked.

'Just a couple of minutes,' she replied and suggested that I sit up and fix my clothes. She wiped my face with a cool damp towel, which made me feel more alert. I began to worry again.

I felt very weak walking up the granite steps of the Dublin hospital, with its tall Georgian facade and massive hall door. The nurse greeted the porter who directed her to the admissions office. She sat me down on a long bench and gave me my chart to keep on my lap. The waiting area was dark and quiet; the only light available came from the sliding glass panels of the admissions office itself.

'Someone will look after you in a minute or two,' she said and prepared to leave.

She brushed my fringe off my forehead with her hand and said that she would see me soon again. I looked at her but didn't speak, then I bowed my head as she walked away.

An attractive, dark-haired young woman came to the window of the admissions office and asked me to come in. She wore bright red lipstick and I couldn't help noticing the length of her fingernails and the fact they were painted to match her lips. I handed her my chart and she copied down the information from it. Every time she smiled, she revealed two rows of pure white, straight teeth slightly stained by her lipstick.

'And you're just nine years of age, Patrick, is that right?' she asked in a refined accent.

'Yes,' I said.

'You're a very big man for nine, and very brave too.'

I forced a smile. I knew I was very small and slight for my age. Then she said I was making a bit of history, as I was the only child in the hospital. She couldn't remember if anyone so young had been admitted before. Because I was the youngest person there, she suggested that I should receive special treatment.

'You don't have any brothers, do you?'

'No.'

'Well I have three brothers who are a little bit bigger than you. They have lots and lots of comics and I think you should have some of them to read while you're with us. Isn't that a good idea?' she asked.

'I don't know,' I replied.

She telephoned to tell a nurse that the patient they were expecting was now ready to go to the ward. I became nervous and began to cry. The receptionist did her best to comfort me with assurances that she would be calling with the comics and that I would get to like the hospital after the first few days.

A nurse came and brought me the short distance to the lift. She slammed its criss-crossed iron gate and pressed the button numbered three. Its sudden movement frightened me and I held her hand tightly until it stopped with a jolt. When the gates opened, I stepped out quickly.

St Patrick's Ward was bigger than any ward I had ever been in. Its high walls were painted two different shades of green with a grey dividing line. The windows were very tall and had ropes to open the top sections. The amount of light getting into the ward during the day was restricted because of shadows cast by other parts of the building which jutted out from the ward I was in. The view from the windows consisted of the back of other buildings, and, looking down, I could see the felted roof of what was obviously a new extension to the hospital. Large fluorescent lights hung from the ceiling, suspended with chains and covered by wide metal shades. They were only switched off on the brightest days and then only for a very short time. The patients were mainly elderly, though there were a few who were probably in their twenties. The coughing and discharging of phlegm into stainless steel cups were sounds I had experienced before; so was the smell of stale urine from uncovered bottles on the floor under some of the beds. What scared me were the painful groans of a man whose bed had been screened off, his voice feeble and tired as he tried to get the attention of one of the nurses. The only evidence of his existence, apart from the groaning, was the sight of a circular glass bottle, inverted and discharging blood into his arm from a T-shaped stand. Patients like him were screened off most of the time, though whenever a nurse went inside their curtains to adjust the flow rate of the drip, I made a point of peeping through gaps to see as much as I could. I was always frightened by what I'd see – a sickly-looking man propped up on many pillows, his arm strapped to a plastic-covered splint to prevent him flexing it where a needle with its tube attached entered his skin. His face would be grey and lifeless, his cheeks sunken and his dull eyes stared from deep caverns framed by black circular lines. Inevitably they died. The entire ward joined the hospital chaplain as he recited a decade of the Rosary for the departed soul.

'He has left this world,' the priest would say, 'and gone to a place where he will experience no more pain, only joy and happiness, eternal life with God and His angels.'

Whenever a death occurred those men who were allowed out of bed took it in turns to pray beside the corpse. They opened and closed the screens gently to avoid making unnecessary noise. Distraught relatives arrived, crying wearily despite the best efforts of nurses and nuns to comfort them. Often wives, their faces distorted with grief, wailed openly and pleaded with the Almighty to give them back their husbands. Grieving sons and daughters tried to console them only to find that they too were angry with the compassionate God who had taken their father. The priest held the hands of the people overcome with pain and grief and reminded them that it was the will of God that their loved one had been taken. During my stay in that hospital I was to witness the heartbreak and the agony of death many times, I was also to become less afraid of it than I had previously been.

Because I was so young, nurses and patients tried to protect me from these scenes. I was given comics to occupy my mind and distract me from what was happening. This practice served only to make me more curious about the subject, and even though I was terrified of dying, I wanted to know what a dead person looked like.

A man died and I asked a nurse if I could go behind the screens and see him, saying that I wanted to say a prayer for him.

She hesitated and then said she would carry me as long as I was sure that I wouldn't be frightened.

'I can walk over,' I said.

'No,' she insisted, 'I'll carry you.'

She lifted me into her arms, asking me not to squash her white triangular veil. I carefully put my hands underneath it and she asked me to make sure I didn't pull it off altogether. I grew tense as I got near to the dead man, and wondered if she could feel me trembling. She opened the screens and from her arms I looked directly down on the man's sunken, marble-like face.

'He's just like he's asleep,' I whispered, somehow realizing that to speak out loud would be wrong.

'Yes,' she said, 'it's like going asleep and never waking again.'

His hands were crossed on his chest and there was a Rosary beads and brown scapular entwined in his fingers. Beside the bed a small table was covered by a white cloth embroidered with a gold cross. A candle burned in its brass holder beside holy water in a brass bowl.

'How do you die?' I asked her as she carried me back to bed.

'Your heart stops,' she said, putting her hand inside my pyjamas' top and holding it gently over my heart. 'Your heart is beating away in there and it will beat for many, many years to come.'

She tucked in the covers tightly over me, then took my face in her hands and kissed me lightly on the forehead before walking away. The tenderness of that moment is something I will never forget.

During my first weeks there I was examined by many students. Mostly they were in groups accompanied by a senior doctor, but sometimes by themselves. At other times it would be one or two students. Such experiences were always embarrassing and seemed devoid of any consideration of how I felt. Bedcovers were literally thrown back, and my clothes removed without anyone ever asking whether I objected. A group of staring eyes pierced my naked body while first one, then a second, third and fourth tried out various examinations, from simply listening to my heart and lungs to holding their hands beneath my testicles and asking me to cough. There was the usual barrage of questions about whether either my father or mother had any form of illness. I didn't know and said so. Brothers and sisters, what about them? I had a sister and told them that she was all right. Foreign students were the most difficult to deal with. Their accents were strange and I had the greatest difficulty understanding their questions. When I did answer, I often had to repeat myself as they didn't appear to understand me. Group examinations often lasted an hour, after which there was practically no part of me left untouched. When they were finished they simply left me behind the screens where I put back on my pyjamas and waited for a nurse to remake the bed.

While in St Patrick's Ward, I was under the care of Professor Casey, an elderly bespectacled man with a deeply wrinkled, kind face. He always smiled at me as he approached my bed flanked by an entourage of students and other doctors, seeking a diagnosis from the students after they had examined me.

He'd pointed out that I had been in three hospitals before this one and that so far there was no positive diagnosis of my condition made. He'd refer briefly to post polio before dismissing it on the grounds that there were none of the symptoms associated with that condition, such as muscle wastage or paralysis.

One morning as his students listened attentively he suggested that there might be some neurological disorder which would take time to ascertain. A biopsy would have to be done and the results closely looked at. He finally said the words I feared most. 'I will be taking him down to theatre in the morning.' As I shivered with fright, he suggested that those interested in furthering their medical careers should be present. Having spoken briefly to the ward sister, the Professor came to my bedside and told me he would see me in the morning.

The greatest fear I had, that of being operated on, was about to become a reality. I wanted to scream but was too terrified to do so. I thought of dying and when asked about going to confession I readily accepted. My old fear of dying returned as I confessed to telling lies and being disobedient to the hospital chaplain. While he was imparting absolution, I wondered if I had told him everything. Somehow surgery and death had become inextricably linked in my mind. I was certain I would die. The years of giving answers which I thought would prevent an operation were gone. The worst thing that could ever happen to me was less than twenty-four hours away.

In the afternoon a nurse came to my bed to prepare me for the operation. She removed my pyjamas' bottom and shaved all the fine hair from my left thigh. As the razor glided over my soapy skin I was trembling so much she had to repeatedly warn me of the danger of being cut. She looked closely at my pubic area and decided it did not require shaving.

There was an elderly man in the bed next to mine who was also going to theatre. More than anything else, he convinced me that not only was I likely to die, but so was he. He dragged out his words as he spoke in a loud thick country accent which I found difficult to understand. He insisted that I join him in saying the Rosary and when he started I had no choice but to answer the prayers.

After tea, signs were hung on our beds indicating that we were fasting.

'Oh 'tis a bad sign when ye have to see the like of that thing being hung on the bed. They starve ye first and then they set about cutting ye up while ye'r asleep.'

'They're not going to have to put me asleep,' I said.

'Sure how can ye have an operation without them knocking ye out? Who told ye that?'

'The nurse did.'

'God bless yer innocence, son, but I'd not believe a word that'd come out of the mouth of them people. They mean well I know, but they don't be telling the truth all the bloody time. They'd say anything to keep ye from asking questions.'

I tried to ignore him, to block out what he was saying. I mistrusted doctors and nurses enough without him adding to it. He kept talking, dragging out the words he wanted to stress.

'Sure they can't go cuttin' anyone open without having them asleep and once they have ye asleep, there's no knowing whether ye'll ever come out of it.'

By that night I was in a terrible state of panic, sweating profusely and crying. I didn't want to believe anything he was saying, yet neither could I believe the nurses, despite their sincerity. When I could not get to sleep on my usual dosage of medication, I was given another dose equal to the first. Despite reproaches from the nurses and protests from other patients, the man beside me continued to pray aloud.

When I woke the following morning my bed was screened off. A nun recited the 'Morning Offering' and the baritone voices of the men responded wearily to her various invocations. Breakfast was being served, I could hear the domestic staff asking patients how much sugar they wanted in their tea and when to stop adding milk. Spoons tapped on eggshells or rang around the sides of cups being stirred. A nurse came through the screens to my bedside carrying a steel dish with a needle and syringe in it. She had cotton wool and a bottle labelled 'ether'.

She helped me to change from my pyjamas into a long white cape which she tied at the back.

'Lie on your side,' she said, 'I just want to give you a little injection.' I lay with the gown up around my waist, tensely waiting for the needle.

'Relax,' she said as she swabbed the area with ether, 'if you relax a bit you won't feel a thing, it's just a little prick.'

She administered the injection and I screamed, feeling the liquid in the syringe penetrate through the muscle in my backside before the needle was withdrawn and the area rubbed again with cold ether.

She asked me to allow her to wipe my face and to see me smiling. I was in no humour to oblige and buried my head deep into the pillow and wept.

The injection had the effect of making me drowsy and my mouth began to dry up. By swirling my tongue about I thought I might be able to create the moisture I so desperately craved. I drifted in and out of frighteningly colourful sleep, hallucinations and nightmares, blue rivers and green skies. Enormous spiders and ants crawled across my body. There was a sense of falling from a great height and being unable to stop.

'Can I have a drink of water?' I asked the nurse who came to check on me.

'You can't have any now, but you can have as much as you want when you come back.'

The fears I held were numbed by drugs, and when the trolley arrived to take me from the ward, I was too doped to be frightened. Two men dressed in light green cotton suits, wearing white cotton caps, and masks over their mouths, lifted me onto the trolley and pushed it to the lift. I heard the gates open and felt the wheels roll across the gap between the floor and the lift. I kept my eyes fixed on the ceiling as I was being wheeled to the operating room.

By the time I reached the theatre, the numbing effect of the drugs had given way to fear. I was alert, frightened and acutely aware of what was happening and being said. By contrast with the corridors outside, the theatre was brightly lit and smelt heavily of disinfectant and ether.

The consultant who was to perform the biopsy came to the side of the trolley and checked my pulse.

'How are you?' he asked.

'All right,' I said, my voice trembling.

'There is nothing to worry about. We'll be finished before we get started.' He laughed.

The intensity of the bright circular light overhead caused me to squint. Doctors and nurses gathered, one indistinguishable from the other, except by their voices, caps covering their heads and masks hiding their faces. A green cloth was draped over my face, reducing the blinding light to a dull shadow.

'Are you all right under there?' the cheerful voice of Professor Casey asked.

'Yes,' I replied.

'You're just going to feel a small injection on your thigh and that will be all. You can sing a song if you like.'

I cried as the injection was given and when I tried to reach my thigh with my hand it was pushed away.

'That's it now,' Professor Casey said, 'no more needles, and just another few minutes then we're finished.'

There was a pause while they waited for the local anaesthetic to take effect before a voice asked if I could feel my thigh being pinched.

'No,' I answered.

Someone gripped my hand firmly as I perspired beneath the cloths that covered my body. I winced as the scalpel made its incision and though I couldn't feel the actual cut being made, I felt a dull pain as my skin was opened.

'That hurts,' I said.

The consultant asked that another injection be given immediately. Nurses and some of the students were encouraging me to sing.

'A person can hardly be expected to sing with a towel over his face,' Professor Casey said.

The cloth was moved just enough to enable me to see directly over my head, it still covered my nose and mouth. I wonder how many people have actually sung 'Kelly the Boy from Killane' while undergoing surgery to the great amusement of all present?

When he was finished Professor Casey held up a glass tube containing my skin steeped in a liquid. 'That's what all the fuss was about,' he said, 'and you're still alive.'

I felt greatly relieved as covers were taken away and I was allowed to sit up and look at my leg. It was covered with a strip of plaster about four inches long and two wide. The skin around the plaster was daubed in a pink disinfectant.

'Will I have to come down here again?' I asked.

'Do you want to?'

'No,' I laughed nervously.

'In that case I won't ask you to,' the consultant said.

On the way back to the ward, I was happy that the doctors and nurses had kept their word. I had not been put to sleep as I feared and began to feel that I could trust them. When I was put back into my own bed I noticed the one beside it was empty.

Being in a ward with a lot of old men had its advantages especially when it came to disposing of fruit or sweets they had been given but didn't want. My bedside locker was a depository for all sorts of things, much of which I never ate. Once a week when the nurses cleaned out the lockers there was always rotting fruit in mine which had to be dumped. I'd remember the times I had prayed for an apple or an orange. Now I had more than I could manage to eat. The only time I refused it was when it was offered to me by the relatives of someone who had died. I was afraid to eat that.

In the evenings I was allowed out of bed for an hour. I had pyjamas that were far too big for me and wore a dressing gown more suited to a small man than a young child. One man I particularly liked was in his early thirties, dark haired, quiet, and an avid reader. He kept a chess board, with pieces in place on top of his locker. I was often amused as he played games against himself, moving the white and black pieces in turn. To me, he was a curious figure who never went to communion or confession, even before he was being taken to the theatre. When I got to know him better and he was teaching me how to play chess I asked him why.

'I'm a left footer,' he said.

'What does that mean?' I asked.

He laughed and at first seemed reluctant to tell me, but I persisted.

'I'm a Protestant,' he said casually.

I was shocked and the harder I tried to conceal it the more obvious it became. I remembered everything I had been told about Protestants not getting to heaven and never being able to see God. I even felt it was a sin to be talking to him. Yet I liked him and he was the person in the ward nearest my own age. I told him about the nun who turned off the radio in the Cork hospital because the patients were listening to a Protestant service.

'You wouldn't want to take much notice of the nuns,' he said.

'Why?' I asked innocently.

'Because sometimes they don't exactly tell the truth.'

I couldn't imagine a nun telling lies and I told him so.

'What about a game of chess?' he suggested to get off the subject.

After just a few moves I asked him if he believed in the Blessed Virgin.

'What's the first rule of chess?' he asked and, when I didn't reply, told me.

'Silence. That's the first rule.'

I remained silent and copied each of the moves he made until the board became congested and he began to pick off my pieces and place them to one side. He suggested that if I really wanted to win, I should start making my own moves. Still utterly obsessed with the fact that this man was a Protestant I asked him if he was going to heaven or hell when he died.

'Haven't a clue and I don't care really.'

'Why don't you believe in the Blessed Virgin?' I asked.

'Because virgins can't have babies.'

'Why not?'

'It's a long story,' he said, 'and when you get older you'll understand.'

My curiosity was aroused and I persisted in trying to get him to answer. He refused and, when I asked why, just said, 'Because it's time for you to go back to bed.'

I waited for the nurse to come with my medication and when she did, I was given two and a half tablets, instead of the usual two. I recognized the phenobarbitone, but not the white half-tablet.

'I usually only get two,' I said.

'Well you're getting two and a half now,' she replied.

'Why?' I asked.

'Because the doctor said so.'

'What's the half one?' I asked curiously and she replied that patients were not supposed to know the names of the drugs they were being given. She was becoming agitated by my constant questioning but eventually told me, before warning me to keep my mouth shut or she would get into trouble.

'What are they for?' I asked.

'What are they for? They're to make you better of course. Now will you for God's sake stop asking questions. Just lie down and go to sleep before I get mad.' As I was going to sleep, I repeated the name of my new drug to myself. I never forgot it.

The first time I actually remember celebrating Christmas was in St Patrick's Ward. I was nine years of age. In the days leading up to it many of the patients were allowed home – some for good, others for a few days. The nurses who were artistic painted seasonal pictures on the large windows of the ward and, in one corner, erected a tree which they spent hours adorning with tinsel and crepe paper streamers. For a few nights before Christmas groups of them, in uniform and capes, visited the wards singing Christmas carols.

The expected arrival of Santa Claus during the night was a new experience to me which I found difficult to believe. It was not that I had ever questioned his existence – I simply hadn't heard of him, or if I had, I couldn't remember. The patients and nurses kept reminding me to get to sleep early or otherwise I would get nothing. Every time I was asked what I hoped Santa Claus would leave for me, I answered, 'An electric train'.

There was little doubt that I was the main focus of attention. No visitor came to see any of the patients without calling to my bed and giving me a bag full of fruit or sweets.

On Christmas Eve I hung a pair of socks on the end of my bed. One of the men gave them to me because they were big and 'Santie would fit a lot more stuff into them'. I was told to clean out my locker, 'just in case he might want to put a few things in there too'. In the night, I heard the sound of shuffling and whispers. Opening my eyelids slightly I saw five or six men and a couple of nurses filling my socks. I pretended to be asleep and, all the time they were there, I never moved.

I woke early next morning and went to the end of my bed to see what had been left there. I tore open a parcel wrapped in colourful paper as patients and staff watched, revelling in my excitement, and pretending the whole business was a mystery to them. Inside I discovered a variety of things: jigsaw puzzles, dinky cars, a train engine with a key sticking out of its side and some lengths of track which, when joined together, formed a circle. I delighted in watching the train go round and round.

'Try the locker,' one of the patients said.

I opened its metal door and an avalanche tumbled onto the floor. Apples, oranges, rolls of sweets and boxes of Smarties. There were boxes wrapped in cellophane paper containing cakes sprinkled with fine white sugar. Someone picked up the items that fell and put them on my bed, which by now was taking on the appearance of a shop counter.

On Christmas Day there was no restriction on visiting. Children were brought to see the parent or uncle they had not seen for months. There were great scenes of emotion and joy as a father clasped his sons and daughters to him and wept. They all brought presents and some even had things for me, colouring books and paints, packets of plastic soldiers and books. I noticed a number of patients sharing a bottle of whiskey between them and as they drank they became more and more high-spirited, singing Christmas songs and pursuing fleeing good-humoured nurses who passed. One man who managed to get his arm around a nurse's waist sang at the top of his voice, 'Give us a kiss for Christmas', and attempted to place his lips on hers, but she turned her head and offered her cheek instead. He protested that it was a 'mean round'.

'Make the best of it,' she said. 'It's all you're going to get.'

As he continued to drink, he became more daring in his approaches to the nurses.

'What about you?' he asked another. 'Any chance of a feel?'

She became angry and reminded him of my presence, and when he said I would have to learn sometime she stormed out of the ward.

'It's just a bit of fun,' he shouted after her, 'and anyway, it's Christmas.' But she ignored him. For a time there was an uneasy silence and I heard some of the men say he had 'gone a bit too far'. He blamed the whiskey. Later in the morning when the nurse returned to the ward, he called her over, saying that he wanted to apologize but she ignored him again. He sat on his bed in misery, the Christmas presents from his family unopened around him.

CHAPTER ELEVEN

At about half past twelve that afternoon, after I had been given my midday dose of tablets, a nurse appeared carrying a bundle of new clothes and told me I was being taken out for the day.

'Where am I going?' I asked.

'Professor Casey wants you to go to his house for Christmas dinner and to play with his children,' she said.

'I don't want to go.'

'Of course you do.'

'I don't,' I said.

'Well you're going anyway, you wouldn't want to insult him after he buying you all these new clothes.'

Realizing I didn't have any choice I allowed her to dress me in a new pair of short trousers, a white shirt and blue jumper. There was also a pair of white socks and a new pair of black shoes.

When she was putting on the socks the nurse noticed that my big toe was bent, cramped down towards the sole of the foot.

She asked me to straighten it but I couldn't, and I told her so. Because of its position it was extremely difficult to get the shoe on. I used to wait until it released and then quickly get the nurse to push it on.

I sat on the edge of the bed for a few minutes, admiring my clothes and savouring their smell of newness. I walked across the ward amazed at how light my feet felt, having been so used to walking with heavy boots. Suddenly, my back arched and I couldn't move – then, after perhaps thirty seconds or so, it released like a spring uncoiling. I was frightened by this involuntary movement, and as I began to worry about it, it happened a second time. I didn't want the nurses to see but one did and rushed towards me. She tried to push me upright but that made matters worse, and eventually she had to carry me back to bed, where she told me to lie down and take it easy for a few minutes. Another nurse joined her as my back relaxed.

'What happened?' she asked.

'I don't know, I was just walking and I couldn't walk any more.'

Then I asked them if I could take off my shoe because it was hurting me.

'My toe just keeps bending inside it and it's sore.'

'Well stop bending it then,' she said.

'I can't, it just keeps doing it.'

They both looked concerned and agreed to mention it to Professor Casey when he arrived to collect me.

When he came into the ward I watched him speaking to the nurses on duty. He looked concerned as one of them demonstrated with the use of her hand and forearm what was happening to my back. Before coming to my bed he was handed a brown bottle of tablets by the nurse.

'I hear you're in some difficulty?' he said to me.

'Just my toe,' I replied.

He took the chart from the end of my bed and said he

was increasing the dose of my 'new tablet'. That would help ensure that my back didn't arch and prevent my toe giving me trouble. He asked if I would be able to walk from the ward to the car.

'Yes,' I said confidently.

I had only gone a short distance when I was forced to stop. Professor Casey urged me to take my time, to relax, everything would be fine. When I resumed walking, I was determined to keep going and not allow my body to be taken over by strange movements over which I had no control. Within the space of a minute, it happened again and I became terrified that this time I would not emerge from the tight grip of the spasm.

'Has this happened to you before?' he asked.

'Once or twice in Kilkenny hospital when I had the splint on my leg.'

'When did you notice it first, since you came to this hospital?' he asked.

'I don't really know,' I replied.

'Would you say it is just since you started on the new tablets?' he asked.

I thought for a moment and told him that I didn't really know.

'We won't worry about that for the moment,' he said as we walked down the hospital steps to his car and introduced me to his three children who were sitting quietly in the back. They were older than me, with probably as much as five years between his youngest child, a boy, and myself. The two girls looked about sixteen and seventeen. I sat in the front seat for the ten-minute journey from the hospital, looking at the various types of houses we drove past on the way. Despite the urgings of their father, none of the children spoke to me and I said nothing to them.

I was desperately uncomfortable in the car. My toe

twitched violently inside my shoe causing me to squirm. I didn't want anyone to notice, but knew they could see me sweating heavily. Professor Casey shifted his gaze from the road to me many times during the journey and each time I tried to give the impression that I was all right.

'Have we far to go?' I asked.

'Another couple of minutes.'

The car pulled up outside a Georgian house with an elegant oak hall door, its brass fittings looking like they had just been polished. A neatly groomed woman opened the door and descended the three steps to the car. She opened the passenger door and embraced me, welcoming me to her home and hoping that I would enjoy the day. The rest of the family got out and, at their father's request, went into the house while his wife and himself enquired whether I could manage the steps.

'I think so,' I said.

I got out of the car with difficulty and waited as the Professor locked it. He walked towards the house and invited me to follow. I couldn't move. His wife offered to help, but he suggested that I be left alone and given time to relax. As I urged my body to move, I noticed the children watching from a front window. This made the situation worse. My body was refusing to do what my brain was demanding. Then Mrs Casey held my hand which had a soothing effect and I relaxed sufficiently to be able to walk up the steps, through the hallway and into a large brightly lit sitting room, decorated with Christmas lights and cards hanging from string over a magnificent white marble fireplace where a fire blazed. The Professor offered me something to drink and I accepted a large cool glass of lemonade. He and his wife had a glass of sherry and before drinking they toasted each other, their own children, and me. Whenever I looked at him he diverted his gaze. I felt uneasy, conscious of being watched, and worried that what he was observing would give him a reason to operate on me again.

The children were curious about what I did in the orphanage at Christmas. Did Santa come? Did we have a party?

There was no Santa, I said, but I did have to serve three Masses and I added that all of us used to get jelly and custard. The boy, who had been silent up until now, said, 'That wasn't much of a Christmas.'

Then I told them about how Santa came in the hospital and they laughed at me pretending to be asleep while the nurses and patients stuffed my locker and the big pair of socks. Mrs Casey said I was right, and laughed too.

'But,' she added, 'I'm certain the real Santa did come once you were asleep.'

During the day I became increasingly uncomfortable as my toe flexed wildly inside my shoe and became sore. When I could no longer tolerate it I asked Professor Casey if I could remove my shoe.

'Certainly,' he said, asking if my toe was still giving me trouble. He reached into his pocket and took out the bottle of tablets he had taken from the hospital, then looked at his watch and remarked that it was a bit soon to take any more. Later in the afternoon when he gave me two I was embarrassed swallowing them while his children watched.

At six o'clock dinner was served. The table was covered in a white, finely embroidered table cloth and at every place there was a cracker, laid out along with an assortment of knives, forks, and spoons. The golden-coloured turkey was placed on a silver tray in the centre of the table, its basted body glistening in the candlelight surrounding it. Professor Casey sat at one end of the table, his wife sat opposite him. I was seated at his right, opposite his son, who offered me a cracker to pull. It broke with a sharp crack which instinctively caused me to duck as paper hats and tiny plastic toys flew into the air. I had never pulled one before and had no idea that the pieces of coloured paper wrapped tightly in elastic bands were paper hats.

The doctor and his family rose to say grace before meals and as I attempted to stand, he indicated that I could remain seated. When grace was finished he reminded his family to remember children like me who didn't have parents or a home for Christmas. I could feel my face redden but kept my head bowed so that no-one would notice.

Everyone at the table wore a paper hat during dinner, and as the adults poured themselves wine, their eldest daughter asked if she could have some. Her father refused, saying she had taken the pledge and couldn't take alcohol until she was twenty-one.

Throughout the meal I felt uneasy and uncomfortable. I was an intruder in a family unit, expected to fit but unable to do so. Everything that went on was alien to me, the food was unlike anything I had ever tasted before. I was confused by the variety of knives, forks and spoons around my plate, never sure which one to use. I was reluctant to try the various sauces which the children spread so liberally over their food. I was afraid to ask for anything and, as they all chatted, wondered if I would always feel so out of place in a family situation as I did that day.

My bare foot was now involuntarily either kicking one of the family or banging hard against the wooden frame of the chair. My paper hat became soggy from perspiration and its dye ran down my face. I wanted to get away from the table and to sit on the floor, where I knew I would be most comfortable.

The room lights were switched off and the candles on the table cast eerie shadows on the walls. Those members of the family still at the table whispered to each other as though some secret ritual was about to begin. I wondered what was happening. From the kitchen I heard Mrs Casey singing 'Silent Night, Holy Night,' her voice becoming clearer as she re-entered the room carrying the Christmas pudding on a plate. On top of the pudding a blue flame danced lightly and the air was filled with the rich smell of brandy. The family joined in the singing as I watched the flame flicker and begin to die away in a stream of blue rivulets running down the sides. There was silence as the flame on the pudding wavered between life and death and when it finally died, they cheered. This was obviously a family tradition to which they attached great importance.

After dinner Professor Casey and his wife sat on the big settee near the fire, drinking from magnificent bulbous glasses. I sat on the floor with their son playing a dice game. They spoke quietly to each other, not realizing I could hear parts of their conversation. She asked her husband had he any idea what I was suffering from, adding that I looked desperately uncomfortable most of the time.

'No,' he sighed, 'but it appears to be progressive.'

'What will happen to him?' she asked.

Again he sighed and said he didn't know. He stood up and reminded me it was time to go. I put away the various pieces of the game and was about to put my shoe on when he said there was no point in wearing a shoe that hurt. Asking his children to remain with their mother and assuring them he would be back soon, he lifted me into his arms and held me as I said goodbye to everyone. It felt very strange to be carried to his car. He settled me into the front seat.

'We'll go for a quick spin into town to see the lights,' he said. It was not a long journey and we didn't speak until we reached the city centre. There were few people about, mostly young couples, hand in hand, or with an arm wrapped tightly around their partner's body. They were dressed to keep out the chill of the December evening with heavy coats, gloves and scarves, yet despite these barriers, there was a sense of real intimacy between them.

O'Connell Street and Henry Street were a mass of brightly coloured lights which were reflected on the windscreen of the car. Whenever we came to a shop window with toys the doctor pulled up close to enable me to have as good a view as possible of the display.

Driving back to the hospital he chatted to me about the hospital. Did I like it? Were the nurses nice to me? What were the other hospitals like and would I like to be able to go back to the school?

'I don't really ever want to go back to that school,' I said.

'Why?' he asked inquisitively.

Without really intending to I found myself telling him about everything that had happened to me there, the beatings by the nuns, the locking up in dark rooms, even how I had fallen down the altar steps while carrying the missal during Mass. He laughed loudly at that, saying it could have happened to a Bishop.

Suddenly I was tempted to ask if he knew anything about my parents. I wanted to tell him about the recurring fears I had of hanging men and of death. I was certain he would believe me. But though I felt very much at ease with this man now, I stopped short of telling him anything about my secret fears. I wanted him to know, not to gain his sympathy, but because I was certain he would understand and believe me. Sometimes I still wonder if he too knew the facts that were hidden from me.

He carried me from the lift into the ward and when one of the nurses offered to help he would not allow her to, saying that I was no weight at all.

Before he left he looked at my chart and told the nurse he wanted the dosage of the new tablet increased immediately and the Phenobarbitone continued with one extra tablet any time I showed signs of distress.

Perhaps it was because I had been with him over Christmas that I felt much more relaxed with him afterwards. One morning early in the new year he checked my foot and noticed the position of my toe.

'Is that the way your toe stays all the time?' he asked.

'Most of the time,' I answered.

'And when is it not like that?'

'When I'm busy doing something, like playing a game or reading.'

He asked the nurse if I was sleeping all right and if there was any movement of my foot while I was asleep. She said there was not.

'Patrick,' he said, 'I am going to have to send you to another doctor.'

I froze with fear and disbelief. This was the man who was so kind and gentle to me, who had introduced me to a family for the first time I could remember. Now he was sending me to another doctor, which to me meant a change of hospital. I didn't want him to see me cry as I told him that I didn't want to go away.

'Who said anything about going away?' he asked. 'You won't have to move hospitals, just wards. That's not so bad. Is it?'

'No.'

'And I'll be able to keep an eye on you, and no doubt some of your nurse girlfriends will come and visit you for the time you are there.'

He pressed his hand firmly down on my head and remarked on the length of my hair. 'We'll have to get that cut for you one of these days, maybe you'll come to the barber with me when I'm not too busy.'

'Where is the other doctor?' I asked nervously.

'Mother of Mercy Ward.'

'Will I have to stay there?'

'That depends on what he says,' he said, adding that he was certain I would be back in his ward sometime.

'Is the other doctor going to be able to make me better?'

'I hope so, after all that's why we are sending you to him, and if he doesn't he will have to deal with me,' he laughed.

I had settled into St Patrick's Ward and didn't want to leave, but by now realized that being moved from place to place was an inevitable part of my life. Despite that, every move was a traumatic one. Even though I had witnessed and experienced suffering during my months there and lived with the seemingly endless visits of the priest to administer extreme unction, I had come to like the place, even love it. Nurses and patients were good to me and treated me as someone special. There were lighter moments, like the empty proposals of marriage which always took the form of a question like: 'How would ya like to put yer shoes under the same bed as meself?'

'You're a desperate man,' the nurse would reply, laughing.

'Desperate! Bejasus I am! You can put that to music.'

CHAPTER TWELVE

Mother of Mercy Ward was a small neurosurgical unit with no more than ten beds. There were two rooms off the corridor reserved for private patients or people recovering from major brain surgery. In contrast to St Patrick's, it was very quiet and the patients appeared to be more ill. Many of the beds were screened off, but every patient I could see had a plaster covering part of his head. Some had their heads completely shaved and covered with a heavy cream-coloured sticking plaster. Their faces were stained by disinfectant running like pink tears down their cheeks and along the back of their necks.

The nurses shifted busily around the ward with no real rapport between them and the patients as there had been in St Patrick's. Whenever I made noise I was reprimanded by a nurse. Patients muttered at me, one elderly man shouting at the nurse on duty to 'get that child to hell out of the place'.

I hated Mother of Mercy Ward, hated its drabness and silence. I hated the cranky old men groaning their way out of the world, though by now I had become so used to death that I accepted the ritual of it as just part of each day. I resented having to stay in bed with no-one to play with.

Some nurses and visitors would bring in comics which I kept stacked in a neat pile at the end of my bed. I never felt comfortable beneath the bedcovers and so I spent most of the day outside them. Whenever the Matron was expected, I was hastily rushed under the covers which were tucked in tightly to ensure that I remained there. It was the same whenever a doctor, priest or nun was visiting the ward, or during visiting hours on Sunday.

My closest friend during those days was a young nun, a novice of barely nineteen or twenty, freshfaced and good looking despite the unattractive habit she had to wear, which only allowed her face and hands to be exposed. Her friendship towards me and the love I felt for her were in marked contrast to my feelings for the nuns in the School at Cappoquin, who by now were nothing more to me than bad memories. I was so used to calling nuns 'Mother' that I found it difficult to address Sister Catherine as 'Sister' for a while. She spoke softly, even when I irritated her by not bothering to learn spellings she had set me. She often asked me to learn pieces out of an old green-covered catechism she had given me and was always pleased when I answered her questions and never angry when I didn't.

One day she gave in to my persistence and had agreed to play a game of draughts with me when the Matron un- expectedly arrived into the ward. She glared icily at the young nun before beckoning to her with her wrinkled finger. Sister Catherine grew visibly distressed as the matron rebuked her for being intimate with a patient. When she reminded the Matron that I had no-one else to play with she responded through her gritted teeth: 'Your job, Sister, is to look after the patients, not to play with them.'

I felt desperately guilty as Sister Catherine wept openly. I wanted to tell her how sorry I was but couldn't bring myself to. It would have been too embarrassing for both of us. As she walked out of the ward accompanied by the matron I wondered if she would ever talk, never mind play with me again.

The nurses wore white uniforms with white veils that hung from their heads like kites. They were heavily starched and held in position with three white hair clips. They wore badges which gave the initial of their first name. Nurse M. Duffy was giving me my medication one day when I asked her what the 'M' stood for. She refused to answer and, when I persisted, said that the patients were not supposed to know the nurses' first names because nurses were not allowed to be familiar with them. Eventually she told me her name was Margaret but warned me never to call her that out loud, or both of us would be in trouble.

'I heard the other nurses calling you Mags,' I said. 'That's what I'm going to call you.'

I teased her and she playfully put her hand across my mouth to stop me. As she did, I bit on the loose skin of her fingers which made her pull her hand away.

'Play a game of Ludo with me, Mags, and I won't call you Mags.'

'I will not,' she said. 'Do you want Drac to catch me?'

'Who's Drac?'

No sooner had I asked the question when I realized she meant the matron. I remembered what happened with Sister Catherine and I understood Margaret Duffy's refusal to play with me.

Not long after I arrived there the consultant neuro-surgeon came to see me. Unlike most of the consultants I had come across during my years in hospital, he didn't have a large group of students with him, just one other doctor. He was friendly towards me and adopted the habit of gripping my nose between the joints of his first two fingers and twisting it gently. It was a gesture designed to make me less nervous of him.

Whenever he wanted to discuss something with the staff of the ward or the doctor accompanying him, he stepped back from the bed and stood in the middle of the ward. Though I could always hear what he was saying I didn't always understand it. But I understood when he told the ward sister he wanted to carry out some investigative surgery and would be taking me 'down' the following morning. I trembled at the mention of the word 'down', which could only mean one thing. I was to be operated on. This time under general anaesthetic. Using his own head as a model he explained to his houseman how he intended to insert plates into my head to be used for various procedures in the future. One would be inserted at the top of my head towards the front and another at the back. He also described the need for 'burr holes' to relieve intracranial pressure. The precise nature of the condition was not clear and the surgery would be purely investigative. Before leaving he twisted my nose and mentioned that he would see me in the morning. I nodded, fighting to hold back the tears.

In the afternoon, Sister Catherine came to my bedside, her face strained as she left a covered tray on the bed-table. She asked me softly not to touch anything as she walked across the ward for screens to put around my bed. Her voice trembled as she said she had to get me ready for the theatre. There was silence between us for a minute before she took a small nurse's scissors from a white leather pouch attached to a belt around her waist. She ran her fingers lovingly through my long straight hair before beginning to cut it. As the scissors snipped tufts of hair into her hand I wept silently and though she did her best to comfort me, I couldn't stop. When the scissors could do no more she unveiled the tray and filled a basin with warm water into which she dropped a bar of soap and a shaving brush, similar to those I had seen many men use to lather their faces before shaving. As the brush soaked, she carefully unwrapped a blade from its paper and inserted it into the open jaws of the silver razor. With a circular motion of the brush on the soap she prepared to lather my head for shaving. At first her movements were jerky as the razor jumped over the longer hair, dragging rather than shaving it. Sister Catherine apologized for hurting me, and replaced the original blade. I touched my head and was shocked by how prickly it felt. Other parts had no hair at all.

The ward sister came behind the screens and asked how Sister Catherine was getting on. She was satisfied with what had been done and wondered if my head felt cold. When I said it did, she suggested I wear a pixie. She left and returned with a green knitted one. She put it on and I threw it to the floor.

'Don't you like it?' the ward sister asked.

'No,' I replied, 'it's stupid looking.'

'Well isn't it better than having nothing at all on your head?'

I kept silent.

'Please yourself,' she said, and left.

Sister Catherine returned to take away the screens. I asked her to leave them.

'Why?' she asked.

'Because I don't want anybody to see me like this,' I sobbed.

'Now be a big man and stop crying, you look fine to me. Nobody is going to laugh at you, I bet they won't even notice.'

She removed the screens. I lay down and wondered if any

of the other patients would notice me. They didn't. Later that evening Margaret Duffy woke me and offered me something to eat. I refused at first and only accepted when she reminded me I would have nothing else before surgery.

'Why did she have to cut all my hair off like that?' I asked in desperation. 'And why do I have to have an operation anyway?'

'Your hair will grow again soon, and the operation is only a very minor one. It'll be all over in a matter of minutes and you won't feel a thing.'

I sat up in bed, very self-conscious of my bald head, and wondering if the domestic staff serving the meal would comment. I tapped on the boiled egg, making only a half-hearted effort to break its shell. I pushed the spoon down and the soft yellow yolk ran down along the eggcup and onto the white plastic plate. One of the men was tearing a slice of white bread into strips and dipping them into his egg, I copied him and enjoyed the taste. Once I had finished eating, a 'Fasting' sign was hung at the head of my bed. My locker was searched for food and any that was found removed. I lay motionless wondering what was going to happen to me and thought of other patients I'd seen coming back from the theatre with tubes suspended from their bodies. I could visualize my face covered in pink antiseptic fluid and my head in sticking plaster. I stared at the young man in the next bed who had been admitted just a few days after me. At twenty-one, he was the nearest of all the patients to me in age – twelve years my senior. He lay flat on his back, his eyes wide open, never blinking, staring at nothing on the ceiling. His life was sustained by liquid food and glucose from inverted glass bottles hanging from drip stands. His urine passed through a plastic tube into a bottle at the side of his bed. At intervals during the day, a nurse checked it and made notes on his chart. From a hole beneath his chin, a rubber tube protruded which drew off phlegm that accumulated on his chest. The sound made by this tube was the most sickening I have ever heard.

On the evening before my own operation I watched as the parents and friends of this young man gathered at his bed, watching and praying that he would come out of his comatose state. His mother had to be supported physically by his father as she wept and wondered aloud why she had ever allowed her son to become involved in rugby.

Vincent Flynn was in a deep coma as a result of an injury he'd received during a game. A scrum collapsed and he was caught underneath. When play resumed, he was left lying on the ground, motionless. It was his birthday. I watched his mother squeeze her son's hand so hard that her own knuckles went pale. It was as though she was desperately trying to awaken him. She looked at me but I turned away, embarrassed at how I looked and ashamed of myself for being caught prying.

When only Vincent's parents remained at his bedside, they knelt and prayed out loud. His father asked me to join in and I did. They recited decades of the Rosary and finally a plea to God to allow their son to be all right 'if it be your holy will'.

Before being given my sleeping tablets, I was checked by a doctor, who listened to my chest and checked my pulse. With a small pen-like torch he looked into my eyes and down my throat. I was tempted to say it was sore, because I knew that could prevent surgery. When he finished and was satisfied about my health, he said he would see me in the morning, in the theatre. That night before going to sleep, I was given more tablets than usual.

I was not allowed to wake properly the following morning. I felt a needle puncture my skin but my senses were too numb to react. Even as I was being dressed in a theatre gown, I made no attempt to resist. I couldn't.

My memories of being placed on the trolley and wheeled from the ward are vague. Most of the images are blurs, foggy scenes involving nurses and hospital orderlies. On the way to the theatre I became fully aware of what was happening as the doping effect of the drugs wore off and I became almost fully alert. Whatever potency that remained in the drugs was nullified by the awful sense of terror within me. I tried to sit up but the strong hand of the orderly pressed firmly down on my shoulder making it impossible to move.

I screamed as I was wheeled into the sterile atmosphere of the theatre where doctors and nurses quickly gathered around in an effort to stop me. Within seconds, my arm was strapped to a plastic-covered piece of wood and a doctor stood over me with a needle and syringe in his hand. The overhead bright circular light hurt my eyes and as I struggled to break free from the people restraining me I felt my right forearm being pierced. A nurse asked me to count to ten. By three the room was beginning to spin, by five I was losing consciousness. I don't remember reaching six.

When I returned from theatre, I was put into one of the small rooms off the main ward. As I came out of the anaesthetic and became more aware I could make out the blurred figure of a nurse sitting beside my bed. I could feel a soreness in my head which I wanted to rub but she prevented me. Every few minutes, her voice reminded me that I was back, and that everything was all right. For the next few hours I drifted from semi-consciousness to unconsciousness, only waking fully when my thirst became unbearable or the pain from the operation overrode the effects of the drugs. I felt the cloth of the sphygmo-manometer being wrapped around my upper arm and tightened as my blood pressure was taken, and then the hissing of air as the pressure was slowly released.

'Water,' I said.

'You can't have water just now, it would make you sick,' the nurse said.

'Water,' I pleaded, through cracked, half-sealed lips.

'You can have all the water you want in a little while.'

I rolled my tongue around my mouth in search of even the slightest sign of moisture, but there was none. The glycerine applied to my lips was no substitute for the drink I desperately craved.

About two hours after returning from theatre a nurse placed one hand at the back of my head and, raising it gently, held a glass of water to my parched mouth. I wanted to gulp it down but she warned that that would only make me sick. When I snatched at it she whisked it away. The next time I got a drink it was to help me swallow pain-killing tablets which were to keep me sedated for the best part of two days.

When I was put back into the main ward I borrowed a small, double-sided shaving mirror from Vincent Flynn's locker. One side gave a normal mirror image, the other side was magnified. It was the magnified side that I chose to look at myself. What I saw horrified me. I was so ugly I wondered how anyone could even look at me. My head seemed to have a big bump on the top where a dressing had been placed after the operation and my face was almost completely pink from surgical antiseptic. I pulled a towel from my locker rail, dipped a corner of it into a glass of water and began to rub my face furiously, trying to remove the pink streaks, but I couldn't make the slightest impression. When I asked a nurse how I could get it off, she said it would fade away itself after a while. Margaret Duffy caught me looking at myself and said that I was being vain.

'I'm not being vain, I just want to see if my hair is growing yet.'

'You hardly expect it to grow two or three days after it has been shaved,' she exclaimed.

'No but I hope I'll have some hair before my birthday.'

'Is that a hint?' she asked, smiling.

'It's my birthday on the nineteenth of May,' I said.

'I thought you didn't know when your birthday was. According to your chart it's not until the nineteenth of June.'

I told her when I was in Kilkenny I'd said it was in February, thinking it might get me out of the room I was in by myself.

'Did they believe you?' she asked.

'No, I don't think so.'

'Do you know what age you'll be?' she wondered.

'Ten.'

'Ten! I suppose we'll have to have a birthday party for you.'

'I suppose,' I answered, unsure what to say. I had never celebrated a birthday before and wondered if a party would be organized for me.

The ward sister asked if I had been to the toilet and when I said I hadn't, she told me I'd need to drink a lot and eat plenty of fruit or they'd have to give me an enema.

The only liquid I had was water and I looked with envy at the array of soda syphon bottles on the other lockers around the ward.

'Why can't I have something like that to drink?' I asked.

There was a bottle of Lucozade on Vincent Flynn's locker, still wrapped in its orange cellophane paper. She unwrapped it and loosened the black stopper with its rubber band from the bottle, remarking how useless it was to Vincent. I felt guilty, as though I was stealing something from someone who didn't even know.

'Can he hear?' I asked.

'No.'

'Can he see?'

'No.'

'But,' I exclaimed, 'his eyes are wide open.'

She told me that Vincent was in a world of his own where everything was dark, just like being in a room where all the curtains were drawn.

'So he's sort of asleep with his eyes open?' I said, and asked her if he would ever wake up. That was in the hands of God she replied. When I asked why he couldn't have an operation to fix him she just said that we would all have to pray and hope for the best.

'Will he die?' I asked finally.

'I think you've had your fair share of questions for one day.'

I asked her why some of the nurses put their finger over the tube sticking out of his throat when they were talking to him. She explained that because of the hole in his windpipe he couldn't speak, even if he wanted to. The only chance of hearing anything he might want to say was by closing off that tube.

'Could I put my finger over it?' I asked.

She looked surprised at first, then lifted me the short distance to his bed. She demonstrated how to cover the tube, warning me never to keep it covered for longer than ten seconds. I was frightened as my finger neared the tube and then touched it. I didn't like the feel of the rubber tube or its wetness at the rim, and was frightened too by the vacant stare of Vincent's dark eyes, like two glass discs that gaped from deep caverns in his boney structured face. His arms were down by his sides, completely straight and still. A breathing corpse.

He was extremely good looking and every morning he was given a bed bath, after which he was shaved with a Ronson electric shaver and his jet black hair was combed back from his forehead. During the day, I was allowed to sit on his bed. In my own mind, I had built up a relationship with him, and made every effort to bring him out of his dark, unconscious world. I spent long periods trying to get him to respond to my voice as I repeated his name. Occasionally I would put my finger over the protruding tube, hoping I would be the first to hear him speak. Whenever I spoke to him I kept my mouth as close to his ear as possible, asking him to blink his eyes if he could hear me, but they remained frozen open.

I always protested at being tucked back into my own bed, saying I wasn't comfortable as my foot was hurting me. By now the bending of one toe had spread to the others and my foot used to cramp so badly I was certain the tendons would snap. Instinctively, I knew that something was going desperately wrong. Whenever the ward sister looked at my foot she reminded me that the neurosurgeon was going to put it right, but it would take time and patience. Gradually the amount of medication I was receiving increased and I didn't bother to count the number of pills I took in a day.

'Why can't I get up?' I asked.

'Because . . .' and she hesitated, 'that is what the doctor says. What's the great hurry anyway, won't it be much better for you to be up when you can walk properly?'

'I don't know if I can walk properly any more,' I said. 'Look at the way my foot is twisted.'

She tried to straighten my toes and turn my foot outwards without causing me pain but she couldn't. The level of involuntary movement from me was so great that she was forced to give up. The bones in my ankle were protruding till they threatened to come through my skin and my foot was becoming increasingly deformed looking. When she said she would have to bring the matter to the attention of the surgeon, I asked if it would mean another operation.

'I don't know,' she answered, 'that will be up to the doctor to decide. Anyway you still have the stitches in from the last time, so it's a bit early to be thinking of more operations.'

My stitches were taken out about ten days after the operation. Margaret Duffy, Sister Catherine and the ward sister drew screens around my bed.

Tiny bristles of hair protruded through the heavy white sticking plaster making its removal difficult and very painful. I cried and tried to stop them pulling it but I was restrained and warned not to touch it because of the risk of infection. With the use of ether, the adhesion of the plaster was broken and it was gradually withdrawn exposing the wound to the cold air. Bloodstained cotton wool pads from my head were tossed into a steel pedal bin.

With their faces masked and rubber gloves on their hands, they began to remove the stitches, assuring me that I would feel no pain. I felt a tweezers pinch and lift the first stitch then with great caution the cold blade of a scissors barely touched my head as it slid under the loop. A snip and it was gently withdrawn and left in a kidney dish on the trolley. There was an air of tension while the procedure was carried out with hardly a word spoken. When it was finished the sense of relaxation among the staff was almost palpable. A small strip of Elastoplast was put over the area where the stitches had been removed. I asked if I could look at myself in Vincent Flynn's mirror, but Margaret

Duffy said I should wait until she had removed all the stains made by the antiseptic from my face. Using a piece of cotton wool soaked in ether, she rubbed gently, taking care to avoid my eyes, nose or mouth. It left my face cold, and its strong smell made me feel drowsy.

When she was finished, she took the mirror from Flynn's locker and held it in front of me.

'Now are you happy?' she asked.

I looked at myself.

'Yeah, I suppose so,' I said.

CHAPTER THIRTEEN

One day when she was not too busy, Margaret Duffy agreed to play a game of snakes and ladders with me. I set out the board as she momentarily attended to another patient. During the game I said I wanted to ask her a question, but that she had to promise to answer whatever I asked. She protested, saying she would make no promises. I persisted, convincing her that the question I wanted answered wasn't a hard one. She agreed to answer.

'Where do babies come from?' I asked suddenly.

She blushed and wondered why I wanted to know.

'I just want to know, that's all.'

'If I tell you, do you promise not to go shouting it around the ward and get me into trouble?'

I nodded. She shook the dice and scaled a ladder on the board with her plastic playing counter.

'They come from their mothers' bellies,' she said, 'now will you throw the dice and stop asking questions.'

'But how do they get in there?'

She reminded me that I'd said 'one question'.

'It doesn't matter anyhow,' I said, 'a boy in the hospital in Kilkenny told me.'

'You tell me then,' she said.

'I will not,' I replied adamantly.

'Have you a boyfriend?' I asked.

'My God, but you are a nosy little demon. What if I have? Is it any of your business?' she mocked playfully.

'What's his name?'

'Mind your own business and get on with the game.'

'Will you buy me a money box?' I asked.

'A money box!' she exclaimed. 'What for?'

'I want to save up to buy a watch.'

'And where do you propose to get the money from?'

'I don't know,' I said, 'I'll just leave it on my locker and maybe when the visitors come they might put something in it.'

'Not only are you nosy, but you're as cute as a fox.'

She laughed and I showed her an advertisement I had taken from a newspaper showing the watch I wanted. It was thirty-two shillings and sixpence.

'I hope it keeps fine for you!' she said, smiling.

I made her promise to get the box the next time she was in town and she agreed.

By visiting time the next Sunday I had my money box placed strategically on my bedside locker and made a point of rattling it to attract attention. There were six pennies in it, given to me by Margaret with the box. 'That's the sixpence,' she said. 'Now all you need is the thirty-two shillings.'

Visitors came over to enquire about what had happened to me. The price of an answer was a contribution towards the cost of the watch. It was a well-worked system. First I told them I was saving for a watch, and when their money dropped into my miniature English postbox, I told them I had polio. If they asked me, as they usually did, if I was getting better I always said no. I would have to have more operations. In most instances this ensured a further donation and a speedy departure of the inquisitor.

It was only a short time before the box was filled and I was confident that I had sufficient money to make my purchase. Getting the money out was a slow, noisy business. I had to insert a knife into the slot and allow the coins to slide out along its blade. The noise irritated the other patients, more than one of whom shouted for a nurse to 'take that blasted box and the child out of here'. The more hatred the men expressed towards me, the more I delighted in annoying them.

When they were reminded that I was only a child they responded by saying that I shouldn't be in the ward. One man suggested that they 'find a ward full of noisy little bastards and put him in there!'

I was anxious to get the watch and nothing would persuade me to wait until my birthday. After much pressure, Margaret Duffy promised to get it on her next day off. I gave her the money and the advertisement and asked her to bring it to me as soon as she got back from town.

'I can't do that,' she said. 'The nurses are not allowed on to the wards in civvies.'

Her day off was one of the longest of my life. I convinced myself that she would forget or lose the money or there might be no watches left when she got to the shop. When she came on duty Margaret Duffy handed me a neatly wrapped parcel. I tore through the wrapping paper and broke open the cardboard box containing the watch. In sheer delight I looked at the dial, the golden figures, the large second hand that moved jerkily around the face. I listened to the ticking before eventually putting it on my wrist. At first the brown leather strap was too loose and it was only with the aid of the pointed blade of a scissors that additional holes were made to allow the strap to be buckled.

I couldn't resist fiddling with the winder, turning it gently to make sure it was wound.

'Once a day is enough to wind the watch,' Margaret said. 'More often than that and you'll wreck it.'

For the first few hours, I kept an almost constant eye on the watch and checked with every nurse that passed by to see if their watches corresponded to my own.

That evening, when the ward was quiet, I took the back off the watch to see what was inside. As I was putting it on again, the second hand fell off. I tried desperately to fix it but couldn't. In exasperation, I left the hand inside the dial and decided to pretend that it fell off while I was asleep.

'Wake up, sleepy head. What time is it?' I recognized Margaret Duffy's voice next morning.

I sat up and looked innocently at my watch.

'I don't know what time it is,' I said, 'I forgot to wind it last night and now it's stopped.'

My voice trembled as I handed it to her and I knew I wasn't going to convince her by my story. I started crying.

'Did you open the watch?' she asked.

'I just wanted to have a look inside. I didn't mean to break it.'

When she saw how upset I was she agreed to take the watch back and try to have it changed, provided I promised to say nothing about having opened it. During her break she took it back, carefully wrapped in paper from a present brought to another patient, warning me before leaving not to expect miracles.

Later in the day she returned to the ward smiling broadly. She took a new watch from the large square pocket of her uniform and helped me to put it on, remarking that they wouldn't replace the strap because it had been tampered with.

That night the ward sister examined the wound on my head by gently lifting the sticking plaster that had covered it since my stitches had been removed. There was no need for a replacement plaster and I could touch my head if I wanted to. By now my hair had started to grow and looked just like a tight crew cut. The self-consciousness of being bald was gone and I was looking forward to having a full head of hair again.

But it wouldn't be that way. The ward sister informed me I would be going to the theatre again. I was shocked and kept repeating that I didn't want to go. It hadn't been long since I was there last.

'Well now,' she said, 'if you want to get better . . .'

'I don't,' I said sharply.

'And I suppose you don't want to go to the Zoo either?'

I looked at her.

'Yes,' she said, 'Nurse Duffy and her boyfriend want to take you out for a day soon, but you can only go if you're good and if Matron agrees.'

'When have I to go to the theatre?' I asked nervously.

'In the morning.'

'How could I have to go? The doctor hasn't even been around and the dressing from the last is just gone.'

She said this operation was the second part of the first one and was only a very minor 'job' not to be worried about. The priest would be around later. The routine was familiar. Notification of an operation. Fear of death while undergoing surgery. Then confession. The cleaning of the soul, just in case.

Again, Sister Catherine was given the job of 'prepping' me. She screened off the bed and apologized for having to shave my head again. 'Someday,' she said, 'it'll be all over.' She lathered my head and shaved it completely, taking great care not to hurt the previous scar which was still tender. Her hand trembled as the razor removed the freshly grown, downy hair.

'Why do I have to have operations on my head?' I asked.

'I wish I knew,' she said with sadness in her voice. I could feel her concern for me. She was so different. She was kind, laughed a lot and played games with me. Lifting me in her arms she would carry me out of the ward, to a garden at the rear of the hospital where she'd take photographs of me, seated on a blanket, in front of a circular flower bed. Her mother used to buy clothes for me and she took great pride in dressing me and ensuring I looked well. I always received my medication promptly when she was on duty and consequently seldom became distressed or overanxious. In the times of my greatest stress she made a special effort to alleviate it, always trying to be there as I left the ward for surgery and again when I returned.

Next morning in the operating theatre, the neurosurgeon greeted me by giving my nose a slight twist. When he asked if I was frightened I didn't bother to respond. A needle pierced the most prominent vein in my arm and within seconds I was drowsy and dizzy. Soon I was asleep and he was making further incisions on my scalp in preparation for drilling through my skull.

Later as the trolley was wheeled back into the ward I was partially awake. Drifting in and out of sleep, I heard the sounds I was familiar with. Men coughing. The news being read on Radio Eireann. Through half-open eyes I could see Sister Catherine walking beside the trolley and felt the softness of her hand firmly gripping mine.

I felt well when I woke, not as sick or as thirsty as I had been previously. The thirst I dreaded so much was speedily vanquished by a cup of warm sweetened tea which Sister Catherine held and allowed me to take at my own pace.

Within a few hours I was sitting up in bed and having a light meal.

I was ten years of age before I celebrated a birthday. Birthdays didn't happen in the Industrial School and were not bothered about in any of the other hospitals I had been in. In Mother of Mercy Ward, there was a certain amount of excitement when anyone was celebrating a birthday. A request might be played for them on Radio Eireann's *Hospitals' Requests*, and there would be more than the usual amount of visitors. It wasn't unusual to see a relative slip a bottle from a brown paper bag discreetly under the bedcovers of the patient he was visiting. For that day nurses turned a blind eye to what was happening, though next morning the half-empty bottle of whiskey would be confiscated after a search of bedside lockers. Wives fussed more than usual and if the opportunity presented itself would draw a screen around the bed, through the folds of which I could see them embrace and kiss their husbands with great passion and urgency.

I woke early on 19 May 1961 to a chorus of 'Happy Birthday' from nurses and some patients. Both night-nurses and day-nurses had gathered around Sister Catherine and Margaret Duffy who were carrying a large parcel. A white envelope bearing my name was sellotaped to it. As it was lifted onto my bed, they asked me to guess what it was, but I was too excited to. It felt light and delicate. As they helped to remove the paper, the shining chrome bars of a birdcage were slowly revealed containing a beautiful, greyish-blue budgie that hopped from perch to perch.

'What are you going to call him?' Margaret asked.

'I don't know,' I answered.

'What about Pedro?' she suggested, pronouncing the 'P' as a 'B'.

'OK,' I said, repeating the name. I was so delighted and

preoccupied with the present that I didn't notice a card pinned on the wall over my bed. It was Margaret Duffy who drew my attention to it.

I looked up at the long unfolded card and read out *PADDY: TEN YEARS OLD*. The words were printed in bright luminous green.

'That was made specially for you,' she said.

'Who made it?' I asked.

'Bernard did.'

'Who is Bernard?'

'He's my boyfriend,' she said, blushing slightly, as she realized she had given his name unintentionally. 'You'll meet him later. You're coming to the Zoo with us.'

I asked to have everything taken off my locker so I could put the cage as close to me as possible. I stared through the tiny rails, my eyes riveted on the bird fluttering around the cage, chirping and occasionally screeching as he hung by his beak from a yellow plastic swing. The noise was annoying some of the patients who were demanding that the ward sister 'take that damned bird to hell out of the place'.

'You should take the bloody child too, and that would solve all the problems,' one shouted.

The Matron arrived as the ward sister was explaining to those objecting that it was my birthday and they should accept the right of a child to have some fun. Matron walked towards me, looking angrily at the budgie. Then the brightly coloured card over the bed caught her eye. She called the ward sister and demanded that the cage be removed from the ward at once.

'We are in a hospital, Sister, not a home for pets,' she said sternly.

The ward sister tried to explain, but the Matron was not interested and said so. I was bitterly disappointed as my present was taken from the ward. Despite my tears the Matron warned me that she didn't want to see the bird back in the ward again or the other patients disturbed.

'What is the meaning of this?' she said, pointing to the birthday card over my bed.

'It's a birthday card, Matron,' the sister replied. 'One of the nurses got it made specially.'

'It will have to come down immediately. It is more like an advertisement for whiskey and it could be upsetting to the older patients.'

She walked swiftly towards the door, turning to warn that she would be back. As the card was removed, the ward sister told me that I could go to her office any time I liked to play with the budgie.

Sister Catherine dressed me in new clothes, saying that she 'wanted her little man to be looking lovely when he went out'. She carried me in her arms out to the garden where she took some 'Birthday Photos'. By this time I had great difficulty in keeping still and became very stressed when having a photo taken. The harder I tried to keep steady, the more difficult it became. She looked at the patch on my head where the hair had not grown since my operation, and suggested that I should wear a hat while out. I thought a hat would look silly and when I told her so, she didn't pursue the matter.

As I waited to be brought out, I wondered how I was going to manage to get around the Zoo. I was worried about travelling in the car, remembering how tense and uncomfortable I had been the last time I had travelled in one. I was confused as to whether I wanted to go or not, but I said nothing.

Margaret Duffy arrived into the ward with her boyfriend Bernard and immediately noticed that the cage and budgie were gone along with the card he had made.

'Where's Pedro?' she asked, angrily. 'And what happened the card?'

The ward sister told her what happened. Margaret was furious and referred to her as 'a right bitch'. She laughed at the thought of the card being an advertisement for whiskey.

Bernard looked on, unsure of what was happening. He was a tall thin man with very sharp features and a pale complexion. He had blond hair and deeply set blue eyes. After we had been introduced to each other the ward sister told Margaret that she had reservations about asking Matron that I be allowed out, in case it would result in a refusal. She suggested that they slip out of the hospital with me as quickly and quietly as possible. Bernard lifted me and carried me down the short corridor to the main hall and out the door into his black Volkswagen. There was a sense of urgency about everything from the time we left the ward until the car was out of sight of the hospital.

When Bernard carried me through the entrance of Dublin Zoo the cashier indicated he would not be taking for me. He suggested that instead of having to carry me around they might like to use one of the buggies lined up just inside the gates. Margaret pulled one out and Bernard put me sitting in it. I was most uncomfortable, my stockinged feet banged relentlessly against the polished steel frame and as my spasms became strong and violent, my feet actually entangled themselves behind the footrests, which could have broken my legs were it not for the swift movements of my companions. Eventually I could no longer endure the pain or discomfort of the buggy. Margaret and Bernard agreed to carry me on a rota basis, and whenever we came to a cage where a lot of people had gathered, she politely asked to be excused. Children asked their parents why I had hardly any hair. Why was I not wearing shoes and why were my feet all crooked? Why did I have to be carried? But the adults and their patronizing smiles were more difficult to cope with than these perfectly understandable questions. Many of them clipped their children around the ear and told them to mind their own business. One child received a tremendous wallop when he said in a loud, musical, Dublin accent, 'Hey Ma, that fella looks like a monkey, his ears stick out and he has a furry head.'

I wanted to get away from the crowds and be alone with Bernard and Margaret. He went to the shop while she carried me to a wooden bench at the edge of a lake. There were just a few people around and I was much more content. The realization that I was being constantly stared at had dampened my interest in the animals, except for a tiger called 'Rama'. Bernard took a photograph of Margaret and me in front of his cage, while in the background the tiger devoured what appeared to me to be a horse's head. The animal's growling was interspersed with the sound of flesh being torn from bone, as the elegant beast held his meal firmly between two enormous front paws.

Bernard returned from the shop and sat to one side of me, sharing crisps, chocolate and lemonade.

'What will you do when Mags leaves?' he said suddenly.

I could feel her jab him furiously in the ribs with her elbow.

I was extremely close to Margaret Duffy and had come to regard her in many ways as a mother figure, someone that I could love, and who would return that love. I had never given a thought to the possibility of her leaving, though deep down I always felt we would be parted by me being moved to another hospital. I was equally attached to Sister Catherine but because she was a nun I felt there was always a barrier between us.

I wanted to be alone with her, to talk. Why was she leaving? Where was she going? Would I ever see her again or would it be just another person I loved and trusted gone for ever from my life?

'When are you going?' I asked eventually.

There was a slight agitation in her voice as she answered. 'I don't know.'

'But Bernard said you were.'

'Look,' she said, forcing me to look her straight in the face, 'it's not as if we'll never see each other again.'

The moment she spoke those words I knew that a close friendship was coming to an end. At first I didn't want to know what she intended doing. I made that obvious by remaining silent on the journey back to her boyfriend's flat. My sulking obviously annoyed her and when I was sitting on a bed she caught me by the hand and shook me slightly.

'Listen,' she said, 'I'm very fond of you, you know that. It's not going to be easy for me to leave. Not only do I have to leave you. What about my parents and my brothers and sisters as well as other friends? Do you think I won't miss them?'

I kept silent while we had tea and cakes. While they were washing up I got off the bed and slid across the floor on my backside. Neither of them heard or noticed me. As I touched Margaret's stockinged leg she screamed, frightened by the sudden and unexpected touch of my hand.

'Why don't you tell me where you're going?' I asked.

She squatted down to be as close to me as possible, then with her eyes fixed firmly on mine she said, 'Bernard and I are getting married and are going to live in America.'

I went hysterical and began to scream and throw things around the small bed-sit. I accused her of liking 'that fella' better than me.

'You're the only friend I have in that smelly, stinking ward full of cross old men. You don't care what happens to me. Do you. Do you?' I screamed at her and when she tried to put her arms around me, I pounded my clenched fists into her chest and tried to kick her. As her boyfriend moved to restrain me, she told him she was all right.

'Sister Catherine is very fond of you, and when I'm gone she will take care of you.'

'I hate nuns,' I said.

'That's not true, and you know it.' She was getting angry. 'Sister Catherine is very good to you. Who gets you all the lovely clothes you wear and who goes to the theatre with you? Isn't she always there when you wake up? She takes better care of you than I ever could and it is not fair to say that you don't like her.'

'I wouldn't have to go to the theatre if she didn't shave off my hair,' I shouted.

'Now you're being stupid. You know well she's just doing what she has to.'

I knew she was right and knew also that whether I liked it or not, I was going to have to let go of her. She had her own life which I could not be a part of.

'Why do you have to leave?' I asked.

'Because I will be finished my training and once I get married I'll have to leave the hospital anyway.'

'Will you ever come to see me?' I asked.

'I'll try, but America is a long way away, and it costs a lot to get home. There's nothing to stop you writing and I will always answer your letters. I'll by dying to know how you're getting on.'

I didn't speak on the journey back to the hospital and as she lifted me from the car, Margaret asked me to say good-bye to Bernard. I grunted something or other and when he pressed money into my hand, saying it was for 'that famous money box' I didn't even thank him. I blamed him for taking Margaret out of my life.

'Are you never going to speak to me again?' she asked as she held my face close to hers, going up the steps of the hospital.

'No,' I growled.

'Not even if I promise to buy you a goldfish and bowl before I leave?'

'That old bitch of a Matron will just take it like she took the budgie.'

She laughed uncontrollably at my outburst. I laughed too. She whispered into my ear that bitch was not a nice word, but that I was right.

That laughter lifted the terrible hatred I felt for her a few hours earlier. When we reached the ward, Sister Catherine and the ward sister brought a sponge cake with ten lighted candles to my bedside. The three of them sang happy birthday and got me to blow out the candles and make a wish. A piece of cake was offered to all the patients, some of whom took it while others refused. While I was eating I stared into Margaret Duffy's eyes and noticed tears in them. She left the cake on a piece of cardboard and rushed from the ward, saying that Bernard was waiting in the car. That was the moment I accepted the inevitability of her leaving for good.

In the days before she left, I made a point of ignoring Margaret Duffy as much as I could and turning my attention and affections to Sister Catherine. I looked to her to play games with me and for praise whenever I did anything.

Sister Catherine was different in every way from the nuns I had grown up with – kind, gentle and not afraid to show affection. She was never cruel to me and when I did require a reprimand, it was usually a playful event, like the day I was being particularly difficult, climbing out of bed and sliding around the ward on my behind. I slid under the patients' beds much to their irritation. She pursued me from bed to bed and suddenly said, 'Here's Drac,' with an urgency in her voice.

I came out from under a bed and was sliding across the floor to my own when she swept me up into her arms. I was laughing as she brought me to an upstairs bathroom and put me sitting in the empty bath, telling me to stay there until I decided to behave myself. She hadn't thought I would be able to get out of it, but within minutes I was at the top of the stairs calling her name. From there I could see into the office where she was busy writing the day report into a ledger. She noticed me and rushed up.

'How did you get out of there?' she asked, lifting me into the office. She put me sitting in a chair at the desk beside her while she continued writing. I couldn't resist the temptation to lift the black telephone and hold it to my ear.

'What number do you want?' a male voice said.

There was a board hanging in front of me with a list of numbers on it and I gave him one.

'Are you a patient?' he asked gruffly.

'Yes,' I said.

'Patients are not supposed to use the phone. Where's the sister in charge of that ward? I want to speak to her immediately.'

I slammed down the receiver, shaking with fear and told her what had happened.

'Did anyone see you using the phone?' she asked.

'Just you.'

'Me!' she exclaimed. 'I didn't see anything.'

If I felt particularly lonely I asked to be put sitting on Vincent Flynn's bed, where I would wave my hands franti-

216

cally at him in the hope that he would blink. When that did not bring a response I tugged gently at his hair and even twisted his nose in the way the neurosurgeon used to twist mine. I used to read Enid Blyton's 'Famous Five' books for him and tell him silly 'Paddy the Irishman' jokes and laugh loudly into his face. Sometimes I'd hold his mirror in front of him.

For months his parents had been calling to see him every evening, but when it became apparent that he was not getting better the visits became shorter and less frequent. Every time I saw them I longed for the love and affection of a mother or father. Indeed many times as I watched them hold their son's hand I used to turn my back so they wouldn't see me crying. They always asked to see a doctor about what was being done for their son and sometimes asked about the chances of a particular operation being successful. I had noticed that when Vincent was being taken to the theatre his father was offered a form to sign which I heard a doctor describe as a 'consent form'. I never saw anyone sign a form for me but often wondered who, if anyone, did. The other thought I had constantly was if I had parents, would they have allowed so much to happen to me?

One afternoon while many of the patients slept, I noticed a change in Vincent Flynn's breathing and called the nurse. She was quickly followed into the ward by the sister in charge, who asked that screens be brought to the bed and his parents be contacted.

The chaplain was at his bedside by the time his parents and family arrived. They gathered in a cluster in the middle of the ward as he prayed aloud in Latin. I found myself responding to prayers I had not said since leaving the Industrial School. It seemed appropriate that mine should be the voice most prominent as he died.

I was deeply moved as his body was taken from the ward. The procession of grieving relations and friends made its way from the ward to the morgue at the rear of the hospital. His death didn't frighten me, though it caused me great sadness. Sister Catherine embraced me, saying that he was better off with God. Her words somehow seemed right.

CHAPTER FOURTEEN

I was starting to lose count of the number of times I had been to the operating theatre. I seem to have the memory of some form of surgery to my head twice in the same week on two occasions. All I can be certain of is that today there are eight scar marks on my skull. Vincent Flynn was dead and Margaret Duffy was gone to live in America. She sent a postcard, saying she had arrived safely, and would write as soon as she settled in. Weeks passed and no letter arrived. Sister Catherine was on duty less and less as she was in 'block', attending lectures in preparation for exams. She was also approaching the time when she would take her final vows which could mean her departure from the hospital.

That summer my head was X-rayed from a number of different angles. A few days later, the neurosurgeon studied the lunar landscape appearance of my brain on the X-ray viewing frame in the ward and drew imaginary circles around different parts of it. He discussed with his houseman what he proposed doing. He told the ward sister that the procedure was difficult, but if it was successful there should be a marked improvement in my condition. He hoped for a reduction in the amount of spasm and a lessening of my dependence on drugs. Intensive care would be essential in the days following the operation, and a close eye would have to be kept for any emotional or physical changes in me. Before leaving the ward, he twisted my nose and asked me to be brave. He ran his hand over my head, feeling the hair which was just beginning to grow. I could sense that whatever he intended doing it was going to be difficult and though I was only ten I didn't share the apparent optimism of nurses and doctors that the operation would be a success. As I worried about what lay ahead, the ward sister reminded me that even though the operation was going to be longer than the previous one, it would be worth it all. Success would mean that I could walk again and be able to leave the hospital.

'Will this be the last time that I have to go down?' I asked nervously.

'That depends on how successful it is.'

'I don't want to go, please,' I begged.

'Now, Paddy,' she said, 'if this operation is successful you'll be able to get up and about.'

'But I don't want to have another operation.'

'Wouldn't you like to be finished with tablets and not to be afraid any more? Wouldn't you like to stop living in wards with old people?'

'I don't mind old people,' I replied.

'Yes, but wouldn't you prefer to be with children of your own age? Your doctor is a good doctor, you have to trust him. All the patients and nurses will be thinking of you and looking forward to seeing you well again.'

I said nothing. I didn't care any more what they did to me. I hadn't the slightest interest in being able to walk or mix with other children. I didn't pray for the success of the operation and only went to confession out of habit. Not even the prospect of death worried me.

In the late afternoon screens were drawn around my bed and a trolley arrived containing the instruments for giving an enema – a white enamel jug containing saline water, wrapped in towels to keep it warm, a basin of water and a bar of soap. On the lower section of the trolley there was a bedpan covered in a blue check cloth, a funnel, a thin length of reddish rubber hose and a jar containing petroleum jelly.

When the bottoms of my pyjamas had been removed, I was told to turn onto my side and bend my knees up towards my chest. My pyjama top was raised along my back and tucked underneath my armpits. I shivered with cold and fear. One nurse held me while a second prepared to administer the enema. I heard the familiar slapping sound of rubber gloves being drawn on and felt a smear of jelly being applied to my anus before my body was penetrated by a rubber tube. As it was being inserted, the nurse told me to shout if it hurt. I managed to look over my shoulder and saw her holding a steel funnel connected to a thin rubber hose, before the first nurse forced my head back towards her. Warm water was poured into the funnel and ran down the tube into me. The feeling was horrible and I wanted to force it back out. I would have only for the constant reminders to 'hold on to it' from the nurses. As more water was poured in the urge to discharge it became unbearable.

'I can't hold it any longer,' I cried.

'Just another minute or two,' they both urged.

I gripped the rubber sheet I was lying on, and clenched my teeth.

'I can't, I can't,' I pleaded.

The tube was withdrawn and before they could get me onto the bedpan, my bowels had emptied onto the rubber sheet. A nurse quickly lifted me off the bed while the other slipped the bedpan beneath me. I was desperately weak and certain I was going to faint. I lay there embarrassed and terrified.

Sister Catherine came to shave my head, a task I'm certain she disliked intensely but had to do. Each time she shaved it there was an extra wound to be careful of where the skin was still delicate and tender.

'Now,' she asked as she finished, 'are you not going to give me a smile?'

'No,' I said.

'Are you still going to marry me?' she asked.

'I don't know,' I replied and asked if she would come to the theatre. Gently, she held my face in her hands and promised to be with me as I was brought down and by my bed when I emerged from the anaesthetic.

I was given a higher than usual dose of drugs on the morning of my operation as well as a pre-med injection which sent me into a deep sleep. I have only the vaguest memories of being changed into a green robe and taken from the ward to the operating theatre. One thing I remember vividly, though, is the number of people that touched me as the trolley passed down the corridor – a series of blurred images on which I tried to focus but couldn't. I felt their hands touching my cheeks or the light pressure of a palm on my forehead. It seemed as though they were in sympathy with me and aware of how serious the surgery about to be performed was.

The scenes within the operating theatre were familiar, eyes gazing down from the strip of skin between the mask-tops and the green cloth caps, each person indistinguishable from the others. I was less nervous than usual due to heavy sedation. Some medical checks were carried out before the surgeon about to perform the operation spoke to me. I ignored him.

A needle pierced my arm and a male voice asked me to

count to ten. Instead of doing so aloud as I usually did, I counted silently. Unconsciously or consciously, I decided to defy the anaesthetic, and by the time I reached eight my eyes were still open and fixed firmly on the bright circular light overhead. Then I felt the needle being withdrawn, and the rubber band on my arm tightened. Fingers slapped on the veins in my forearm, to make them more prominent and easier to inject. The needle was reinserted and, without bothering to count, I passed out.

Years later, one night on BBC radio, I heard an actual recording of a neurological procedure similar to that which I underwent. Naturally I cannot describe the operation I was involved in in 1961 and am not attempting to do so. But it was with an extraordinary sense of terror and fascination that I sat listening to the voice of the surgeon, identifying with the aid of carefully marked X-rays, the area of brain he wanted to deal with. The patient's head was completely daubed and then marked where incisions were to be made before being covered with a sort of artificial skin, a strong, stretchy plastic which clung tightly to his scalp. Cuts were made in it, giving access to the skull and eventually the brain itself. Incisions were held open by surgical clips known as retractors, and dressings were inserted into wounds to absorb any bleeding that occurred before veins could be tied off. The microphones picked up the surgeon and anaesthetist in constant conversation, checking pulse rate and blood pressure as well as deciding when the level of anaesthesia needed to be deepened or reduced. Gradually the hard bone of the skull was exposed as the openings became wide and deep.

For the surgeon to reach the brain it was necessary to cut and drill through the skull. It is a manoeuvre requiring great skill and dexterity. As the drill sank deeper, the patient's head vibrated and had to be held steady. The sound of the drill boring its way deep into the skull was shrill and piercing. As one drill bit became less effective it was replaced by another resembling a tiny rose, each petal a small spike. Any bone that could not be removed using a drill was cut out with a fine-toothed saw which made a screeching sound as it cut. Bone filings dispersed during the excavation process were collected and mixed with silicone for replacement on completion of the operation. Veins and arteries close to the site where the surgeon wished to extirpate tissue considered responsible for the patient's condition were carefully closed off, and the utmost care taken in the removal of the tissue. There are many complications to this type of surgery, some of which include anxiety, depression, apathy and bronchial pneumonia.

Listening to the programme brought back the most traumatic event of my own operation, when I woke while apparently still being operated on. Absolute confirmation of this is difficult to obtain, but my memory of the event is sharp and clear. I was conscious of everything that was going on around me. The overhead light hurt my eyes momentarily and I could see the surgeon and other theatre staff looking at me. I was aware of various pieces of equipment close at hand and, most clearly, I remember that awful parched feeling in my mouth. 'Water,' I managed to say before being put back to sleep.

Many hours later I was taken from the operating theatre and put into intensive care. A nurse kept vigilance at my bedside and I remember her being instructed not to leave me alone for a minute and to ensure that I didn't sneeze or become distressed in any way.

I was kept asleep for nearly two days before being moved back to one of the rooms off the ward. I heard Sister Catherine's voice telling me that everything was fine. Slowly and painfully I emerged from the anaesthetic to discover my arm tied down while I was given a blood transfusion. I tried to lift my head to take the water being offered me, but it was too painful to do so. Sister Catherine dipped a cloth in the glass and I sucked on it instead.

During the next days I suffered great pain in my head and also developed the severest pain I have ever experienced in my chest. I gasped and screamed, convinced that I was about to die. I begged Sister Catherine not to let me and she promised she wouldn't.

She looked at me with great anxiety as she damped my flushed face with a cloth, suggesting in desperation that I try to think of nice things. She said the doctor would come soon and everything was going to be fine.

'I don't want to die,' I screamed again.

'You're not going to die,' she said, her voice trembling. When the doctor came into the ward, I was still distressed and screaming. He listened to my chest and placed his hand on my forehead before prescribing medication and stressed the need to keep me under constant observation.

I have a very vivid memory of a woman standing in the doorway. I looked at her as she stared pitifully back and, despite the severity of the pain, I clearly remember her walking towards my bed and asking Sister Catherine if it would be all right for her to stay and say a few prayers.

They both knelt and continued to pray even when the neurosurgeon returned briefly to the room. Sister Catherine rose and listened to him as he spoke quietly. The woman moved away and leaning against the wall, prayed continuously, running her fingers along black Rosary beads. After the doctor left she handed a brown scapular to Sister Catherine and insisted that she put it around my neck.

I do not know who this woman was, whether she was even real or just the ghost of a fevered imagination, nor do I know the significance of the brown scapular, apart from its reputed curative abilities. I can say with absolute certainty that following this event I went into a deep sleep and when I woke the excruciating pain in my chest was gone.

After about a week, I was taken back into the main ward. It must have been obvious to the doctors and nurses that the operation which they expected so much from was a failure. My toes twitched relentlessly and the degree of spasm in my body had greatly increased. I had no control whatever over the movement of either leg and most of the time they were contracted tightly against my chest. My toes bent so much and the spasms in my feet were so intense that they badly strained the tendons in my ankles which added greatly to my discomfort.

In August 1961, I was taken from Mother of Mercy Ward and returned to St Patrick's from where I had been taken nine months previously. The impact of this move on me was devastating and distressed me more than any previous one.

Sister Catherine's attempts to console and reassure me were futile. I screamed in protest as she carried me from the ward, unable to believe her when she told me I would be back. Under such stress, the ferocity of my spasm was so great that Sister Catherine had to protect herself from being injured by the uncontrollable kicking action of my legs. When I was put to bed in St Patrick's Ward, steel rails were erected on each side of it to prevent me falling out. It was the final indignity.

As she left the ward I shouted after Sister Catherine not to go. She returned to my bed and promised she would do everything possible to ensure I wouldn't have to stay in there.

In March 1962, I was taken back to Mother of Mercy Ward, for what the hospital records describe as 'possible basal ganglion surgery'. The record goes on: 'A small abscess had formed around one of the previous markers and therefore no surgery could be done, but the marker was removed'.

By now Sister Catherine had left to work as a missionary nun in Kenya. I couldn't understand why, though I accepted the inevitability of her departure from my life. There was no nurse in the ward that I recognized and the only familiar face was the neurosurgeon passing through. My biggest worry was that I would have to undergo more surgery and every time I saw him I could feel my entire body tense. He often came to the end of my bed but said very little to me. He had even given up twisting my nose.

I no longer bothered trying to get out of bed and became so withdrawn that I took little notice of anything going on around me. The excitement and fun of Margaret Duffy and Sister Catherine had left an enormous gap in my life. Now the days seemed longer, and though the nurses were kind and caring there was a distance between me and them which I had no desire to remove.

During my final days in that hospital preparations were made for a visit by an East German Cardinal. Every time the nurses tucked me into bed I climbed back out. I couldn't bear the feel of the sheets on my feet and when the prince of the church arrived I was outside the bedcovers.

Perhaps because I was the only child in the ward, he came directly to my bed and extended his hand for me to kiss his ring. Press photographers followed, taking pictures that would be included in the following day's papers.

A photograph from one shows his thumb making the sign of the cross on my forehead. My feet are clearly visible, deformed and obviously in spasm and my newly grown hair is sticking up. What the photographs do not show is the sudden, vivid memory I had, when his ringed hand touched my skin, of the day six years before when my uncle's car halted with a jerk at the door of the school and the hands of Mother Paul, white against the blackness of her habit, beckoned me slowly into her care.

Shortly afterwards, on 25 April 1962, I was discharged from there. After many enquiries from doctors on my behalf the only medical records I have been able to obtain are three single pages. On the two of them that give details of surgery the column for 'Next-of-kin or Responsible person' has been left blank. The section of the record referring to where I was discharged to reads: '—FD/SH Home'.

I was in fact sent to another hospital.

EPILOGUE

I was moved to St Mary's Hospital Baldoyle also known as 'The Little Willie Hospital'. The first thing I noticed on entering the hospital was a poster of 'Little Willie'; a small boy, his legs in calipers and his body supported on crutches. The image of this child, who was a patient there, was used extensively to raise funds.

I was put into a ward where the other patients were all about the same age as I was. The hospital at Baldoyle was situated near the seafront close to the racecourse and when the weather was fine 'walks' were organized there. Because of my condition and the extent of my involuntary movement I had to be strapped into my wheelchair. I enjoyed these outings, especially when I was allowed to roll around on the grass. It reminded me that the thing I missed most about being unable to walk was the feel of cool grass under my bare feet. I was not used to sandy beaches and disliked the feel of sand, especially when it got anywhere near my toes.

Two things in particular pleased me about St Mary's in Baldoyle; it had no operating theatre and there was an obvious absence of doctors. A consultant did visit the hospital once a month and anyone requiring surgery would be transferred to another hospital. I was taken to the physiotherapy department every day where efforts were made to straighten out my legs. Often my spasms were so violent that the physiotherapist had to enlist the help of other people to help her hold my legs down. The discomfort I endured during this process was great and I often begged them to let me go. 'Just another few seconds, it's all for your own good,' was the inevitable reply. This effort they put into trying to get me to walk was the worst aspect of my stay there. My legs had to be forcibly straightened, before iron calipers and heavy black boots could be put on me. I was then brought to the walking bars and made to stand between them and look at myself in a full-length mirror. All their efforts were pointless and eventually I was put into a wheelchair and given just the lightest of physiotherapy. Once a week I was allowed into the swimming pool where I was less tense and could feel my muscles relax. However, every time I was instructed to 'kick' I could not. I desperately wanted to but the more I willed my limbs to respond, the more difficult the task became. The frustration was so great that at times I cried.

While in this hospital, I was prepared for confirmation and brought to the local parish church where Archbishop John Charles McQuaid of Dublin confirmed me a 'Soldier of Jesus Christ'. During the ceremony I paid more attention to the altar boys than to anything else. They were moving silently and elegantly around the altar just as I had done five or six years previously. Now I was seated in a wheelchair outside the altar rails, trying to restrain my legs from banging against its metal frame. I had not been in a church since I was admitted to hospital, now the smell of incense, the sounds of the organ and the Latin prayers I had so often responded to brought me back to Cappoquin. I remembered the day I tripped while carrying the missal and coming to in the sacristy, having fainted during Mass. Unbelievably, Mother Paul's voice sounded in my ear as though she was standing beside me. 'You will never set foot inside the rails of an altar again.' Her prophecy had become a reality.

I attended a school in the hospital. It was a fragmented education as I was often taken from the class to the gym. In school I was given the task of teaching the tin whistle to a small class. I had just started learning it before leaving Cappoquin and was able to manage the scale and just one tune, which everyone learned: 'The Dawning of the Day'. The payoff was when the hospital band played this tune on *The Imco Show* on national radio.

I knew that my stay in Baldoyle would be short – I was there for about nine months – and looked forward to being moved to St Mary's Hospital at Cappagh in Finglas, County Dublin. Reports reached Baldoyle that Cappagh was a better hospital, that the nurses were nicer and the nuns were not as cross. It was also a hospital for big boys.

The move to Cappagh was not in the least traumatic as I had prepared myself for it. It was to be a move of great significance to me and one which would undoubtedly have a massive impact on my future. In the first few weeks I underwent surgery to both legs, the purpose of which was to release the tendons at the back of the knee, allowing them to be straightened with greater ease. The surgery was only marginally successful and the surgeon under whose care I was placed recognized this. He actually told me that I would not have to undergo any more surgery. Instinctively I felt I could trust this man, there was a sincerity in his words I had not noticed before in any of the hospitals I had been in.

As I settled into Cappagh and began to make friends I became a more relaxed person. The days of anxiety and tension were fading and I no longer worried about dying. I was surrounded by lively teenagers instead of old people.

Younger boys made plans during the day to raid the convent orchard in the evening, while older lads would try to persuade one of the female patients or a young nurse to meet them at the back of the congress altar, which was used to celebrate Mass every Sunday. This structure had been positioned on O'Connell Bridge in Dublin in 1932 before being moved. It was not unusual for three or four boys with varying degrees of handicap to meet there in the evening for a smoke. Dates with girls were also arranged and it was behind this altar that I got my first kiss. I was now a teenager growing up in an institutional environment but I was happy. I was forging strong relationships with other boys and experiencing the intensity of teenage love. I was enjoying life and being treated as a young adult by nurses and nuns.

One extraordinary event occurred in Cappagh when I began to answer Mass again in Latin, from my wheelchair. The responses to the prayers were still so clear in my mind that I never used a card or missal. I became the hospital altar boy. I was also involved in the Scout Movement and went on regular camping trips to the Dublin Mountains. As my self-confidence continued to grow, my disability somehow seemed irrelevant.

During one of many frequent trips to Lourdes – always paid for by someone hoping I would be cured – I was befriended by a priest. His curiosity about me led to the second meeting between my sister and myself. For her it was to be a traumatic affair. She had last seen me running and walking at seven years of age. Now I was confined to a wheelchair. She still finds it difficult to understand what happened to me in those short years. Many adult years would have to be spent trying, if it was possible, to make up for the lost years of childhood.

I had an interest in music and was tutored in piano by an

occupational therapist attached to the hospital. I hated the lessons and tried every ploy to get out of them. I wanted a guitar and finally managed to buy one. I must have banged out the chord of C thousands of times before doing the same with D. The surgeon under whose care I was, listened, unknown to me, as I sang 'What Have They Done to the Rain'. He clapped and said: 'If The Searchers ever get to hear that, Doyle, you could end up in jail.' He arranged music lessons for me and paid for them himself.

Nurses were becoming more than just people who looked after patients, they were friends. Two or three played a particular role in my life and one determined its course. She gave me real love, both physical and emotional, and I was able to return it. Sometimes it was difficult for me as a teenager to unscramble love from caring. Could a nurse many years senior to me actually love me, and could I love her? I never wanted to be loved out of a sense of duty or pity, I wanted to be loved for the person I was.

During these years I grew into a strong and confident young man. There were no stresses on me and as a result my physical condition improved considerably, even to the extent that for brief occasions I was able to walk without the aid of crutches or calipers.

I forged a particularly strong relationship with two other boys my own age, and it was not unusual to see the three of us, in the company of three nurses, heading for the bus and a day in the city. The nun in charge of our ward was particularly instrumental in ensuring that we went out. Often she called me aside and gave me money, suggesting that I spend it on something other than cigarettes. This nun, now dead, came to my defence when I was caught in the girls' ward, replying, when told by another nun that I was sneaking down to visit a particular girl whenever I got the chance, 'I bet you did a bit of it in your own day, Sister.'

I was introduced to a social worker and the possibility of my being discharged became a regular topic of conversation. These talks 'primed' me for leaving Cappagh and when the day came I was desperately sad and uncertain about the world I was heading into. I had been in institutional care for most of my life, now I was being discharged from hospital to become part of a family.

I was placed with a most wonderful family. A woman with seven children ranging in age from four to fourteen, was prepared to treat me as one of the family, though I found difficulties in getting used to being part of such a unit. I was actively encouraged to visit Cappagh and to get on with my schooling. I was never made to feel different because I was disabled and I was taken with the family on their annual holidays. There was never a problem about making space for one other person or a wheelchair in the grey Borgward Estate. It was from this family that I gained the confidence necessary to feel I could take my place as an equal in society.

There was an inevitability about my departure from the security of a family. I wanted to challenge life. I wanted society to accept me as I had been accepted by others. I moved into a flat on my own while still at school. The flat was my 'house', there was a sense of ownership about it and I could bring people in when I liked without feeling I was intruding on anyone.

Exactly half the welfare payment I received went in rent for the flat, the rest kept me on a diet of cornflakes, eggs, sausages and bread. There were times when the flat was a lonely place. I wrote a little when I couldn't afford to go out or didn't feel like visiting anyone.

Synge Street Christian Brothers School was nearby and I used to push myself to school each day. I particularly enjoyed those years. I was regarded as 'one of the boys' and loved not only the companionship it brought but, most of all, the respect – not pity – I was given by my fellow pupils. Because I had no basic education I found it difficult to deal with certain subjects in school, particularly mathematics, but one teacher determined that I could get a leaving certificate if I was prepared to work hard in and outside of school. He was right. I passed – though only after a recheck of the maths paper.

By the time I left school I was nearly twenty years old and anxious to get a job. I was involved in a relationship which I hoped would result in marriage and so when the offer of a job in CIE was made to me, I grabbed at it. It was a bad decision, though it took twelve years to realize, by which time I felt my very sanity was being threatened. By the time I had the courage to leave, I was moving towards writing and trying to find out about my past. These ventures, uncertain though they were, have proved stimulating, frightening and rewarding.

In 1974, I got married. Many objected to the idea and voiced their total disagreement to a disabled man marrying an able-bodied woman. People took my wife aside and warned her that she would end up 'looking after' me. What infuriated me most about these interfering busybodies was their blatant disregard for the good sense of either my wife or myself. A half-hysterical matron summoned her student nurse to her office and demanded to know 'what was the meaning of it all?' People would ask my wife what sort of sex life she could expect. There were times when the pressure almost caused the relationship to collapse. I began to ignore people who interfered, realizing the futility of talking to them about something which ultimately was none of their business. When all else failed I'd tell them simply to 'fuck off'. This may have been crude but it certainly had the desired effect.

In September 1976 we went to an auction for 'A Victorian House – needing redecoration'. We had looked over the house which had been empty for ten years and, though it was damp and dusty, we decided to try and become the new owners. Our bid was the highest and the auctioneer's hammer came down with the words: 'Sold, to the gentleman seated for seven thousand pounds.'

Looking for a house loan and dealing with solicitors delayed us from actually taking possession until six months later. But on a dark, wet Good Friday evening a car and trailer drove up through the overgrown and neglected front garden, carrying all our belongings. My first child ran around the house amazed at its size. My wife, who was pregnant for the second time, stood in the middle of a bare, dusty and damp room. She held the brass hall door key in her hand and remarked: 'Well, at least it's ours.'

Behind the house a high-speed diesel-engined train hooted as it rushed past, replacing the hissing and panting sound of the steam engines I had been so used to as a child. Looking out the bay window, I fleetingly remembered St Michael's Industrial School. I am typing these words in that same room where trains and granite walls are as close to me now as they were thirty years ago in Cappoquin. I had never been loved there. I am here.

GALLOWAY STREET
John Boyle

'FULL OF HUMOUR IN THE MIDST
OF GRINDING POVERTY'
Lesley McDowell, *Scotsman*

John Boyle was born and raised in Paisley, son of poor
immigrants from the West of Ireland. In this acclaimed
memoir, he tells the story of his childhood, beautifully
capturing the poverty and the rough humour of the streets
he grew up in, and the poignancy of growing up Irish
in Scotland, never quite sure where you belong.

'COMPELS COMPLETE ATTENTION BECAUSE
EVERYTHING HERE, DOWN TO THE LAST FULL
STOP, HAS BEEN CAREFULLY CONSIDERED . . . A
PRECISE AND DEEPLY MOVING EVOCATION OF THE
VANISHED IRISH IMMIGRANT WORLD THAT ONCE
FLOURISHED IN SCOTLAND. IT IS SO GOOD, INDEED,
IT ESTABLISHES A BENCHMARK OTHER MEMOIRISTS
WILL HAVE TO STRIVE VERY HARD TO REACH.
AND OF ITS MANY ACHIEVEMENTS, SURELY THE
MOST IMPORTANT OF ALL IS THAT *GALLOWAY
STREET* DESCRIBES A MISERABLE CHILDHOOD
WITHOUT A SHRED OF SELF-PITY'
Carlo Gèbler, *Irish Times*

'*GALLOWAY STREET* MAY NOT BE MOMENTOUSLY
DRAMATIC, BUT IT IS GENTLY EVENTFUL,
ILLUSTRATING HOW IT'S REALLY THE LITTLE THINGS
THAT ULTIMATELY CHANGE OUR LIVES'
Mark Robertson, *The List*

'SHARPLY OBSERVED . . . POWERFUL AND,
OFTEN, FUNNY'
Albert Smith, *Irish Independent*

0 552 99914 8

BLACK SWAN

EMPTY CRADLES
by Margaret Humphreys

In 1986 Margaret Humphreys, a Nottingham social worker and mother of two, investigated the case of a woman who claimed that, at the age of four, she had been put on a boat to Australia by the British government. At first incredulous, Margaret Humphreys soon discovered that this woman's story was just the tip of an enormous iceberg. As many as an estimated 150,000 children had in fact been deported from children's homes in Britain and shipped off to a 'new life' in distant parts of the Empire – the last as recently as 1967.

Many of the children were told that their parents were dead. Their parents, too, were often deceived; many believed that their children had been adopted in Britain. The reality was very different: for numerous children it was to be a life of horrendous physical and sexual abuse in institutions in Western Australia and elsewhere.

Margaret Humphreys reveals how she gradually unravelled this shocking secret; how she became drawn into the lives of some of these innocent and unwilling exiles, how it became her mission to reunite them with their families in Britain, and how her lonely crusade led to the founding of the Child Migrants Trust.

Empty Cradles is a strong indictment of government, as well as charitable and religious organizations. It is a sad, harrowing story that will move the reader to anger and tears. Yet it offers a message of hope to all the victims of a shameful scandal that has been ignored for too long.

'A scandal that makes *All The President's Men* pale into insignificance . . . brought tears to my eyes'
Terry Waite, *The Times*

'A truly astonishing, haunting, real-life detective story'
She (Australia)

'The secrets of the lost children of Britain may never have been revealed if it had not been for [the actions of] Margaret Humphreys'
Sunday Times

0 552 14164 X

FINDING PEGGY:
A Glasgow Childhood
by Meg Henderson

Scottish journalist Meg Henderson grew up in Glasgow during the fifties and sixties as part of a large and often troubled family. The tenement block in which they lived collapsed and they were moved to the notorious Blackhill district, where religious sectarianism, gang warfare and struggles with hostile bureaucrats were part of daily life for the people. Meg was born into a mixed-religion family, where there was warmth and laughter as well as conflict. She had a close relationship with her mother, Nan, and her mother's sister, Meg's Aunt Peggy, two idealistic, emotional women who took on the troubles of the world. Together they shaped Meg's life, shielded her from the effects of her father's heavy drinking and helped her to move on, eventually, from the slums of Glasgow.

A hopeless romantic, Peggy searched for a husband until late in her life and then endured a harsh, unhappy marriage until she died tragically in childbirth. Her death devastated the family and destroyed Meg's childhood, but it was only as an adult, after the death of her own mother, that Meg was able to discover the shocking facts behind Peggy's untimely demise.

'Beautifully written and immensely enjoyable. Captures Glasgow perfectly with no rose-tinted glass'
Alan Taylor

0 552 14185 2

A SELECTED LIST OF FINE WRITING
AVAILABLE FROM CORGI AND BLACK SWAN

99065 5	THE PAST IS MYSELF	*Christabel Bielenberg*	£7.99
99469 3	THE ROAD AHEAD	*Christabel Bielenberg*	£7.99
99914 8	GALLOWAY STREET	*John Boyle*	£6.99
14493 2	THE JIGSAW MAN	*Paul Britton*	£6.99
14718 4	PICKING UP THE PIECES	*Paul Britton*	£6.99
99926 1	DEAR TOM	*Tom Courtenay*	£7.99
14239 5	MY FEUDAL LORD	*Tehmina Durrani*	£6.99
99802 8	DON'T WALK IN THE LONG GRASS		
		Tenniel Evans	£6.99
13928 9	DAUGHTER OF PERSIA	*Sattareh Farman Farmaian*	£6.99
12833 3	THE HOUSE BY THE DVINA	*Eugenie Fraser*	£8.99
14760 5	THE CUSTOM OF THE SEA	*Neil Hanson*	£5.99
14185 2	FINDING PEGGY: A GLASGOW CHILDHOOD		
		Meg Henderson	£7.99
99930 X	THE MADNESS OF ADAM & EVE	*David Horrobin*	£8.99
14164 X	EMPTY CRADLES	*Margaret Humphreys*	£8.99
14595 5	BETWEEN EXTREMES	*Brian Keenan and John McCarthy*	£7.99
13944 0	DIANA'S STORY	*Deric Longden*	£6.99
13943 2	LOST FOR WORDS	*Deric Longden*	£5.99
14544 0	FAMILY LIFE	*Elisabeth Luard*	£7.99
14594 7	STILL LIFE	*Elisabeth Luard*	£6.99
13356 6	NOT WITHOUT MY DAUGHTER	*Betty Mahmoody*	£6.99
13953 X	SOME OTHER RAINBOW	*John McCarthy & Jill Morrell*	£6.99
14276 X	IMMEDIATE ACTION	*Andy McNab*	£6.99
14137 2	A KENTISH LAD	*Frank Muir*	£7.99
14288 3	BRIDGE ACROSS MY SORROWS	*Christina Noble*	£6.99
14632 3	MAMA TINA	*Christina Noble*	£5.99
14607 2	THE INFORMER	*Sean O'Callaghan*	£6.99
14763 X	HIGH SPIRITS	*Joan Sims*	£6.99
54654 2	HIS BRIGHT LIGHT:	*Danielle Steel*	£5.99
	The Story of my son, Nick Traina		
14814 8	TOMORROW TO BE BRAVE	*Susan Travers*	£7.99
14767 2	. . . AND JUNE WHITFIELD	*June Whitfield*	£6.99
99891 5	IN THE SHADOW OF A SAINT	*Ken Wiwa*	£7.99